Copyright ©

The Best Dating advice for older women

Discovering Love's infinite possibilities after 40. An essential guide with proven strategies for finding love in your 40s 50s 60s and beyond.

By

Taylor B Butler

Copyright ©

Copyright ©Taylor B. Butler 2023. All rights reserved.

Before this document is duplicated or reproduced in any manner, the publisher's consent must be gained. Therefore, the contents within can neither be stored

Copyright ©

Table of contents

Chapter 1
Embracing Your Age and Self-Confidence in
Importance of self acceptance
Dating While Following Your Life Experience
Knowing the Special Chances of Dating as an Older Woman

Chapter 2
Overcoming Obstacles and Addressing Age-Related Concerns
Addressing Age-Related Concerns
Dealing with Societal Stereotypes and Common Misconceptions
The following are frequent fallacies and preconceptions regarding older women in the dating world, along with methods to dispel them:
Overcoming Rejection Fear

Chapter 3
Dating Protocol and Etiquette
Presented as a dating metaphor for older women, Modern Rules
Guidelines for Older Women Dating:
Rules for dating older women
Typical blunders on a first date

Copyright ©

Chapter: 4
Setting Priorities and Goals for Your Dating Life
Deciding what you truly want and refusing to accept anything less
Reevaluating Relationship Objectives and Keeping Partnership and Independence in Check
Balance of Independence and Partnership
Managing Expectations

Chapter: 5
Effective Listening and Empathy
Assertive Communication Techniques
Navigating Difficult Conversations
How to interact with a prospective partner when out on a first date

Chapter 6:
Dating Techniques for Various Relationship Objectives
Socializing and Casual Dating
Finding a Long-Term Partner
Examining Non-Traditional Relationship Models

Chapter 7:
Sexuality and Intimacy
Regaining Intimacy
Examining Sexual Health and Safety
Building Emotional Bonds

Copyright ©

Chapter 8
Understanding that beauty is determined by confidence and self-care rather than age
Personal well-being and self-care

chapter 9
Dating while parenting
Discussing Dating with Your Children
Introducing Your Children to a New Partner
Parenting responsibilities and dating obligations must be balanced.
Here are a few realistic instances that show how an older woman may juggle dating and parenting responsibilities:

Chapter 10
Building Step-Relationships and Blending Families
Creating Positive Bonds with Adult Children
Common Strategies for overcoming it

Chapter 11
Dating After a Divorce or Loss
Understanding the Dynamics of Step-Parenting and Blended Families

Chapter 12
Early Recognizance of Red Flags
Telltale Symptoms of a Toxic Relationship

Copyright ©

Recognizing the signs of emotional abuse, emotional manipulation, and potential money diggers
Finding Prospective Gold Miners
Symptoms of toxic relationships in advance and advice for avoiding them
How to break up with a toxic partner

Chapter 13
Advice for older ladies on online dating
Engaging Messages and Navigating Online Conversations real-world examples.
How to recognize bogus internet frauds with examples of how to do so
Safety Measures for Online Meetings with Strangers

For older ladies seeking for a lifelong spouse, here is one more bit of advice

Copyright ©

Introduction

Once upon a time, a lady by the name of Grace lived in a little community tucked away by the sea. In her early sixties, Grace was a bright and graceful lady who had lately come to a turning point in her life. Her surprising re-single status came after years of devoting herself to her profession and establishing a family.

Grace was first confused and doubtful as she attempted to navigate the dating scene. If she was too old to fall in love again or if the dating scene had moved on without her. A glimmer of hope, though, blazed brightly in her heart. Age was simply a number, and she was aware that anybody may find love at any stage of life.

Grace happened to come upon the book "The best dating advice for older women: Discovering Love's infinite possibilities after 40 " one fateful day. She

Copyright ©

chose to go through its pages out of sheer curiosity. Grace had a growing feeling of strength and opportunity with each new chapter she read. She became inspired by the accounts of women who overcame hardship and later in life found love.

Grace concluded that the secret to finding love rested in accepting her timeless beauty and wisdom as she read the counsel and insights given in the book. She discovered that the wrinkles on her face were signs of a life well lived, and she learned to embrace them. She also learned to dress with inner confidence. Breaking free from the restrictions that society had imposed on elderly women, Grace started to reinterpret social expectations.

With her newly found confidence, Grace entered the world of online dating. She learned useful techniques from the book to establish an engaging and genuine online presence. She created a profile

Copyright ©

that reflected her lively personality, her love of art and adventure, and the essence of her special soul.

Grace discovered the value of establishing boundaries and putting self-care first thanks to the advice of "The best dating advice for older women ." She engaged herself in pursuits that nourished her well-being and provided her pleasure. Grace welcomed life's experiences, finding satisfaction and a greater sense of self in each one, whether it included taking long walks along the beach or enrolling in a painting class.

Grace's perspective changed as each day went by. She attracted men with her magnetic aura, setting up fun dates with honest talks and sincere relationships. Although there were ups and downs along the way, Grace faced them with grace and resiliency because she knew she was worthy of love, esteem, and company.

Copyright ©

Age is nothing more than a number in a universe where love has no bounds. Dating at a certain age is no longer subject to the outmoded stereotypes and preconceived assumptions of society. More than ever, older women are enjoying their autonomy, experience, and the thrilling quest for love in their later years. "The Best Dating Advice for Older women; " Discovering Love's Infinite Possibilities After 40".An essential guide with proven strategies for finding love in your 40s, 50s , 60s and beyond.
Is your compass, pointing you in the direction of the life-changing opportunities that lie ahead if you are an older woman looking for a lively, meaningful love adventure.

This book, which is equal parts narrative and professional guidance, is a glimmering ray of hope for people who think that love has no time limit. It emphasizes the distinct advantages and skills older women bring to the dating scene while also recognizing their inherent attractiveness and charm.

Copyright ©

This book is your dependable friend whether you're a divorcee looking to rekindle romance, a widow navigating the murky seas of love, or a single lady preferring to enjoy the company.

You will find a gold mine of dating advice on these pages, from seasoned relationship specialists, psychiatrists, and inspirational older women who have bravely started their own spectacular dating experiences. You'll discover that becoming older is not a drawback but rather a badge of pride, a monument to a life full of life lessons, insight, and fortitude. The strength of self-assurance, genuineness, and maturity as the cornerstones of fruitful dating are acknowledged and celebrated in this book.

"The Best Dating Advice for Older Women . "Discovering Love's infinite possibilities after 40".An essential guide with proven strategies for finding love at your 40s 50s 60s and beyond, offers

Copyright ©

you the opportunity to travel with Grace and a host of other remarkable women as you set off on your adventure. Let's acknowledge and honor the wisdom, tenacity, and courage that older women bring to their experiences. As you write your own unique love story and embrace a future full of timeless love and lasting relationships, this book will inspire you to embrace the limitless possibilities that lie ahead.

Copyright ©

Chapter 1

Embracing Your Age and Self-Confidence in

We will discuss the importance of accepting your age and gaining self-assurance as an older woman in the dating world in this chapter. We acknowledge that starting a dating life might seem intimidating, but we want to reassure you that this is a wonderful new chapter with the possibility of finding love, friendship, and joy.

Recognizing the Beauty and Value of Aging:

As an older woman, it's crucial to embrace your age. Your remarkable journey is reflected in every wrinkle, gray hair, and experience you have. You have conquered obstacles, reached your objectives, and gained knowledge along the way. Accepting your age means accepting the whole you, complete with all the experiences and memories that have

Copyright ©

helped you become the extraordinary person you are today. By accepting your age, you exude an unrivaled charm and confidence.

Building Self-Confidence:

We are aware that confidence might sometimes wane, particularly when first entering the dating world. But we want you to know that you have amazing talents and capacities. You are a strong lady with a plethora of information and life experiences to give. The first step in developing self-confidence is realizing your value and enjoying your trip. Take pleasure in your accomplishments and who you are as a person. Keep in mind that you have earned the right to be confident while dating and to stand tall.

Embracing Your Life Experience:

Your life experience is a goldmine of knowledge that distinguishes you. It's time to appreciate the value your journey has added to your dating encounters and to embrace their depth. You are an interesting and captivating person because of your experiences, lessons learned, and unique viewpoints. You may connect intimately with people and provide a depth of knowledge to your relationships

Copyright ©

when you accept your life experience. Your life's events have made you the amazing lady you are now, and they should be honored.

Keep in mind that now is your chance to shine. The road of self-discovery and love has no bounds, and age is only a number. We urge you to step into your authority, take pleasure in your age, and develop an inner sense of self-confidence as you begin this new chapter. The whole world is eager to see the beauty of the extraordinary lady you are. Let's go off on a path of empowerment, development, and rewarding connections together.

Self-Acceptance's Influence on Dating:

For older women in particular, self-acceptance is a key component of a successful dating life. It serves as the cornerstone upon which sincere connections and significant relationships are constructed. When you accept and love yourself, warts and all, you exude attractive confidence that draws others to you and fosters genuine relationships.

Self-acceptance in the dating world refers to acknowledging and accepting your special features, both emotional and physical. It involves accepting your age, your life experiences, and all the other aspects of who you are. True self-acceptance challenges social conventions that may uphold artificial beauty standards and overemphasize youth. It's about realizing that you are far more valuable and desirable than your outward look.

When you are confident in who you are, it attracts others to you. You exude confidence from the inside, not from looking for approval from others. Potential partners are attracted to your sincerity and a true sense of self by this contagious confidence in you.

You may establish healthy boundaries and make decisions that are consistent with your beliefs and preferences when you have self-acceptance. You can choose partners that value and respect you for who you are by entering into relationships with a clear understanding of who you are. You get the strength to seek relationships that nourish and complete you when you embrace who you are, as opposed to settling for less than you deserve.

Additionally, self-acceptance promotes relational vulnerability and emotional closeness. Your ability to establish a secure foundation for emotional connection with people depends on your ability to

Copyright ©

embrace all of who you are, including your flaws and prior experiences. Your prospective partners will be more inclined to reciprocate when you are open, which will result in a deeper and more satisfying relationship.

When dating, practicing self-acceptance also entails letting go of self-criticism and rejection anxiety. You embrace yourself with warmth and compassion rather than focusing on your perceived defects or anxieties. This self-compassion turns into a compass that helps you approach dating with a cheerful attitude and fortitude. It allows you to deal with rejection and disappointments gracefully because you are aware that you are not defined by the thoughts or deeds of other people.

Copyright ©

Importance of self acceptance

The importance of self-acceptance in dating ultimately comes down to your capacity to embrace your individuality, radiate confidence, and attract mates who love and appreciate you for who you are. By embracing who you are, you start a path of self-awareness and love, which enhances your dating life and creates the foundation for satisfying and deep interactions. Embrace your uniqueness, celebrate it, and see how the power of self-acceptance changes your dating experience.

Building Confidence When Dating:

For older women in particular, self-confidence is a crucial quality when it comes to negotiating the dating scene. Your ability to present your authentic self, draw in perspective companions, and establish sincere bonds are all made possible by your inner power. Developing self-confidence entails accepting your value, highlighting your advantages, and embracing powerful beliefs that advance your dating life.

Copyright ©

Recognizing your value is the first step in developing self-confidence. You are a great person with a distinct set of skills and life experiences. Recognize the value you provide to a relationship and accept the truth that you deserve to be loved and happy. Keep in mind that becoming older does not make you less valuable; rather, it gives your character more depth and complexity. Accepting this reality creates the ideal environment for real self-confidence to grow.

Second, highlighting your advantages is essential for boosting self-confidence. Make a list of your successes, skills, and admirable qualities. Concentrate on your unique traits and be proud of them. Recognize that your qualities, such as intellect, humor, compassion, or resilience, are advantages in the dating scene. Your self-confidence will radiate outward when you emphasize and value your strengths, which will increase your appeal to possible partners.

Moreover, developing self-confidence requires adopting powerful beliefs. Confront any self-limiting thoughts and self-talk that could be getting in the way of your development. Replace doubtful

Copyright ©

thoughts with positive affirmations of your competence and value. Have faith in your capacity to handle dating with poise and resiliency. Positivity attracts others to you when you embrace empowered ideas, creating opportunities for deep relationships.

Furthermore, pushing yourself outside your comfort zone is a great approach to developing self-confidence. Accept new challenges and take calculated chances when it comes to dating. This may include striking up discussions, going to social gatherings, or investigating internet dating services. By demonstrating to yourself that you are capable of managing novel circumstances and welcoming personal progress, each step you take outside of your comfort zone helps to boost your self-confidence.

Finally, taking care of oneself is essential for fostering and preserving confidence. Put your health—physical, emotional, and mental—first. Take part in joyful pursuits, work on self-compassion, and surround yourself with inspiring people. Taking comprehensive care of oneself improves your self-perception and lays the groundwork for healthy self-confidence.

Copyright ©

In conclusion, developing self-confidence in dating entails realizing your value, highlighting your accomplishments, embracing powerful ideas, moving outside of your comfort zone, and engaging in self-care. You give yourself the ability to negotiate the dating scene with honesty, resiliency, and grace by adopting these behaviors. Keep in mind that self-assurance is alluring and compelling. Building your self-confidence will make it easier for you to connect with possible companions who value and adore the amazing person you are.

Dating While Following Your Life Experience

Your life experience is a priceless asset that distinguishes you from other singles and enhances your dating life. By completely accepting it, you may go into dating with a feeling of maturity, self-assurance, and a distinct viewpoint that can improve your relationships with others.

Copyright ©

Embracing your life experience may have the following benefits for your dating efforts:

Genuineness and Self-Knowledge:
The events in your life have molded you into the person you are now. You get a greater awareness of who you are, your beliefs, and your goals by accepting your path. Your ability to express your real self in relationships and attract partners that value you for who you are as a person is empowered by this self-awareness.

Meaningful Conversations:
You have a multitude of anecdotes, perceptions, and lessons from your experiences. Your discussions with prospective partners will be richer when you embrace your life experience. You may participate in in-depth conversations on a range of subjects, express your viewpoints, and forge deeper connections. Your life experiences provide you the ability to present a distinctive viewpoint and encourage intellectual and emotional relationships with others.

Copyright ©

Psychological Maturity:

Life events often foster emotional development and toughness. You have encountered difficulties, overcame setbacks, and learned from your mistakes. Your ability to negotiate relationships with more empathy, understanding, and compassion is facilitated by your emotional maturity. You are better able to speak, manage the ups and downs of dating, and support your partner on their path.

Embracing your life experience gives you a feeling of confidence and self-assuredness that will help you in your dating pursuits. You have experienced a variety of things and have always emerged stronger. Because of your tenacity and certainty, you make a desirable spouse. With the knowledge that you are capable of handling whatever comes your way, you may approach new relationships with serenity.

Knowledge and Direction:

Both you and your prospective partners may benefit from the knowledge and direction that comes from your life experience. Based on the lessons you've learned, you may provide insightful advice. You can make wise choices, establish sensible limits, and deal with difficulties successfully because of your

Copyright ©

intelligence. You start to serve as your partner's source of support and direction, building a bond based on mutual learning and understanding.

By embracing your life experience, you add a special depth and richness to your dating experience. Your emotional intelligence, self-assurance, knowledge, and genuineness offer a solid basis for developing enduring relationships. Keep in mind that your life experiences have made you into the amazing person you are today; thus, they should be honored and shared with others. Accept your life experience and use it to direct you into relationships that will be meaningful and satisfying.

Knowing the Special Chances of Dating as an Older Woman

Being an older woman and dating offers special options that should be embraced and investigated. You may approach the dating scene with confidence and positivity by being aware of and taking

Copyright ©

advantage of these changes. Here is how to take advantage of these special opportunities:

Self-Assurance and Clarity:
You probably feel more confident and clear about what you want in a relationship now that you are older. Your beliefs, objectives, and deal-breakers are better understood. When you are aware of who you are and what you have to offer, you can go into a dating situation with confidence.

psychological maturity and Stability:
These traits develop as people mature. You've probably acquired insight into what constitutes a good and satisfying relationship, improved your communication skills, and got a better knowledge of your emotions. You can negotiate the dating world with elegance, healthily resolve disagreements, and forge stronger relationships with possible partners thanks to your emotional maturity.

Your life experience and wisdom are significant resources that may enhance your dating life. You provide a plethora of information, experiences, and viewpoints. Your life's events have made you into a complex person with a distinctive view of the world.

Copyright ©

With your possible partners, this breadth of experience may promote interesting talks, mutual learning, and emotional ties.

Independence and Autonomy:
You have probably developed a strong feeling of independence and autonomy as an older woman. Your own life, job, and personal interests have all been developed. Because of your freedom, you may approach partnerships voluntarily rather than out of need. You are free to look for a friend who will enhance your life rather than define it.

A Change in Priorities:
As we become older, our priorities often change. You could feel less pressure to live up to social norms, which will free you up to concentrate on what matters most to you. You may put deeper connections, common ideals, and emotional compatibility ahead of outward appearances. More genuine and satisfying relationships are made possible by this change in priorities.

Regard and understanding amongst people:
Older women often have a strong sense of regard for both themselves and other people. Your

Copyright ©

relationships are more likely to appreciate open dialogue, empathy, and respect for one another. The foundation of trust and understanding built in this way may pave the way for deep and meaningful interactions.

You may approach dating as an older woman with a good attitude and confidence if you comprehend and embrace these special prospects. Recognize your age-related benefits and capabilities and make the most of them. Accept and value your confidence, emotional maturity, life experience, independence, rearranged priorities, and the ability for respect. By doing this, you open the door to satisfying connections with others who share your values and bring pleasure and companionship into your life.

Copyright ©

Copyright ©

Chapter 2

Overcoming Obstacles and Addressing Age-Related Concerns

You could have age-related worries and stifling attitudes as an older woman entering the dating arena, which might restrict your success. We will address these worries in this area and provide helpful suggestions to help you get over them, giving you the confidence to go through the dating world with optimism and self-assurance.

Challenge Stereotypes:

Age and dating stereotypes and prejudices are often upheld by society. It's important to dispel these myths and understand that they do not describe your value or attractiveness. Recognize that age has no bearing on attractiveness, appeal, or compatibility and that many people enjoy and admire the distinctive attributes that come with maturity.

Copyright ©

Concentrate on Inner Beauty:

While outward looks may deteriorate with age, inner beauty always remains. Your kindness, intelligence, compassion, and confidence are all aspects of your inner beauty, so emphasize and cherish them. Develop self-care habits that will improve your general well-being, such as looking after your physical health, participating in activities you like, and fostering your emotional and spiritual well-being. When you emphasize your inner beauty, it emerges and develops into an alluring trait that draws sincere relationships.

Recognize that dating as an older woman comes with various objectives and life experiences. Embrace your stage of life. Accept and be honest about your life stage with prospective partners. By doing this, you may eliminate people who might not be a good fit for you or understand your objectives and goals. Accepting where you are in life enables you to meet like-minded people who value the special traits and experiences that come with experience.

Confidence in Communication:

Copyright ©

In every relationship, good communication is essential. Gain self-assurance while communicating your preferences, limitations, and expectations. Be forthright and truthful about your goals and the qualities you look for in a mate. Put the focus on your life experience and the insightful perspectives you contribute to discussions. Confident communication builds a foundation of understanding and fosters meaningful relationships.

Celebrate Your Age:

Consider your age a badge of pride rather than a restriction. Acknowledge the knowledge, resiliency, and personal development that come from life experience. Accept the assurance and self-assurance that only experience can deliver. Keep in mind that your age is a special advantage that distinguishes you and makes you an interesting and appealing person. People will be attracted to your positivism and self-acceptance if you celebrate your age.

Support Yourself:

Surround yourself with a network of encouraging friends, relatives, or a group of people who share your views. Look for organizations or social groups that appeal to senior singles and provide chances to meet others with comparable experiences and interests. Having a support network will encourage you, provide insightful advice, and serve as a reminder that you are not traveling alone.

By addressing age-related issues and dispelling stifling notions, you give yourself the ability to approach the dating world with confidence and sincerity. Keep in mind that your age is not a disadvantage but rather a special asset that adds to your charm and charisma. Take pride in your inner beauty, speak with confidence, and surround yourself with positive people who value and celebrate your age. With a positive attitude, you may successfully navigate the dating scene and create opportunities for fruitful partnerships.

Copyright ©

Addressing Age-Related Concerns

Change Your Perspective:
Instead of seeing aging as a barrier, change your perspective to emphasize the traits and principles that are important in a relationship. A successful relationship is built on the principles of compatibility, common interests, emotional resonance, and respect for one another. By emphasizing these elements, you break free from social norms and open yourself up to the possibility of real relationships based on substance and compatibility.

Learn from the Past:
You have a plethora of information and lessons learned from previous relationships as a result of your life experience. Make the most of these encounters as educational opportunities that will help you improve your dating preferences and identify dating habits that may no longer be beneficial. Think back on what you've learned and

Copyright ©

use what you've discovered to shape your future decisions.

Accept New possibilities:

You have the benefit of a larger variety of dating possibilities as an older lady. Accept the opportunities that technology presents, such as senior singles-specific online dating services. These online dating services might put you in touch with more compatible companions who value and share the same things as you. Be willing to investigate other opportunities, such as social gatherings, interest organizations, or volunteer work, to meet new people. Taking advantage of new possibilities increases your likelihood of meeting suitable companions.

Have confidence in your experience and appreciate the worth of the unique viewpoints you may contribute to a partnership. You are now a well-rounded person with a plethora of tales and perspectives thanks to the experiences you've had. Have faith in your ability to communicate these experiences with prospective partners since they may promote better understanding and stronger relationships. Your life experiences give your conversations more depth and complexity, which makes you an enticing and compelling partner.

Embrace Self-Compassion:
No matter your age, it's normal to have periods of vulnerability or self-doubt. Remind yourself that you deserve to be loved and happy and practice self-compassion. Be nice to yourself and accept the dating experience as a process of personal development. Celebrate each accomplishment and take lessons from any failures you encounter as you go, treating yourself with tolerance and kindness.

Seek Professional Support:
If your dating experiences are still being hampered by age-related worries or limiting attitudes, you may want to think about getting advice from a therapist or dating coach. These experts can provide insightful advice, support you in overcoming any emotional obstacles, and give you tips on how to develop confidence and resilience. Your ability to overcome obstacles and approach dating with newfound hope will be aided by their knowledge.

You may navigate the dating scene with assurance and enjoyment by facing age-related worries head-

Copyright ©

on and developing a positive outlook. Keep in mind that your age is a strength, not a drawback. Accept your

Dealing with Societal Stereotypes and Common Misconceptions

It may be frustrating and detrimental to your confidence to date as an older woman because of societal assumptions and prejudices. You can overcome these obstacles and negotiate the dating scene on your terms, however, if you have the correct mentality and techniques. Here are a few strategies for addressing and dispelling social stereotypes:

Recognize that cultural prejudices are often founded on constrained perspectives and antiquated assumptions. By accepting your value and the special talents you bring to the table, you may increase your self-confidence. People can see that

Copyright ©

you are not limited by age-related preconceptions when you exude confidence.

Educate and Advocate:

Seize the chance to inform people about the various dating experiences and viewpoints of older women. To clear up misunderstandings and improve understanding, share your own experiences and ideas. By speaking out for yourself and others, you help dispel conventional norms and promote a more welcoming dating scene.

Spend Time with Supportive People Who Value and Celebrate Your Journey as an Older Woman in the Dating World.

Surround Yourself with Positive Influences. Find communities, social networks, or online discussion forums that provide a secure setting for adult singles to meet and exchange experiences. Creating a support system of like-minded people who encourage and support you may help counterbalance the harmful signals that society sends.

Accept Your Unique Story:

Your life experiences have molded you into a complex person with a distinctive tale to tell. Accept

Copyright ©

and confidently tell your narrative, emphasizing the knowledge, development, and resiliency you have attained along the way. Owning your story allows you to disprove stereotypes and highlight the depth of your experiences.

Place a greater emphasis on compatibility and connection by turning your attention away from cultural norms and quick judgments.

Instead, place more emphasis on a person's compatibility, common beliefs, and genuine connection while dating. A successful and meaningful relationship that defies cultural norms may be built by looking for individuals that value you for who you are.

Keep Yourself True

Remain faithful to your own goals, objectives, and limitations. Refuse to compromise your principles or give in to social pressures to fit into a certain mold. The relationships you attract admire and respect you for who you are when you embrace your honesty.

Celebrate Success Stories:

Copyright ©

Look for and highlight examples of successful partnerships with older women. Embrace a supportive environment that challenges preconceptions. By emphasizing these triumphs, you help people understand that finding love and happiness is possible at any age and encourage them to keep going despite prejudices.

Develop your resilience in the face of social prejudices and probable rejection by practicing resilience.

Remind yourself of your value, remain committed to your objectives, and have a positive mindset. Recognize setbacks as chances for development and learning while keeping in mind that the ideal spouse would value and celebrate you for who you are.

Social prejudices and widespread misunderstandings must be dispelled by fortitude, confidence, and tenacity. You may succeed in the dating scene by bucking preconceptions, embracing your individuality, and being loyal to who you are. Keep in mind that you can change society's standards and construct your own story. Take advantage of the dating chances that come with becoming older, and allow your true self to show through to attract mates

Copyright ©

who will admire and celebrate you for the extraordinary person you are.

The following are frequent fallacies and preconceptions regarding older women in the dating world, along with methods to dispel them:

Error: It is a myth that older women are less appealing or beautiful.

Overcoming Strategy: Focus on self-care, celebrate your attractiveness, and embrace your self-confidence. Face down social beauty standards while embracing your uniqueness.

False belief: Older women are helpless or in need.

The best way to overcome this is to emphasize your independence and show that you are self-sufficient. Make it clear what you want and what you expect

Copyright ©

from a relationship by demonstrating that you want it to be mutually beneficial.

Myth: Older women have too much baggage or unresolved difficulties from previous relationships. Reframe your life events as opportunities for learning and personal development as an **overarching strategy**. Describe how they have helped you become more emotionally adept and able to form stronger connections.

Misconception: Older women are reluctant to change and are set in their ways.
Overcoming Strategy: Demonstrate your flexibility and willingness to try new things. Show that you're open to trying out new interests, philosophies, and viewpoints.

Misconception: Older women lack excitement or have low energy levels.
Overcoming Strategy: Demonstrate your vigor and joie de vivre. Take part in activities that excite you to show that you care about developing yourself and trying new things.

Copyright ©

Myth: Older women only need security or stability in their financial situations.
Overcoming Strategy: Clearly express your priorities and core principles. Express that you are not just interested in financial security but also emotional connection, compatibility, and similar ideals.

Misconception: Older women are incapable of or uninterested in sexual exploration.
Overcoming strategy
Celebrate your sensuality and accept your sexuality without feeling ashamed as an overriding strategy. Show that you value closeness and connection by being upfront and honest about your wishes and limits.

Misconception: Older women aren't as digitally savvy.
Overcoming Strategy: Demonstrate your technical prowess and adaptability. Show that you are at ease using online dating services and conversation.

Misconception: Older women lack excitement or are uninteresting.

Copyright ©

Overcoming Strategy: Showcasing your adventurous and busy lifestyle. Discuss your interests, travels, and desire for fresh information. Defy the stereotype by displaying a lively and daring personality.

False belief: Older women are less receptive to learning or development.
Overcoming Strategy: Show that you are dedicated to developing yourself. Showcase your intellectual curiosity while pursuing new interests and continuing your education.

You may fight cultural prejudices and build deep relationships based on respect and understanding by confronting these beliefs head-on and living genuinely. Keep in mind that you may reinvent what it means to be an older woman in the dating market, making your age a strength.

Misconception: Older women aren't as exciting or daring in bed.
Overcoming strategy
Defeat this stigma by embracing your sexuality and having honest conversations with your spouse. Show that passion and closeness can flourish at any age by

Copyright ©

expressing your wants and doing new things together.

Misconception: Older women don't want to create families or have kids.
Overcoming Strategy: Express your preferences and aspirations honestly and assuredly. If having children is not your top priority, let them know that you are happy with your profession, your level of personal satisfaction, or the connections you already have.

Myth: Older women need a provider and are reliant on them financially.
Overcoming Strategy: Emphasize your financial stability and independence. In your pitch, make it clear that you're not only interested in a business relationship; you also want one built on similar values, emotional compatibility, and mutual support.

Myth: Older women are too used to their routines and hesitant to change them.
Overcoming Strategy: In relationships, demonstrate your adaptability and readiness to make concessions. Show that you can change with the

Copyright ©

times, and be willing to compromise and work with your spouse to find a solution.

Misconception: It's a myth that older women aren't capable of or interested in experiencing love and romance.

Overcoming Strategy: Display your ability to be passionate and romantic by expressing your wants, making romantic gestures, and encouraging emotional closeness. By exhibiting a romantic attitude and fostering close relationships with your spouse, you may defy the stereotype.

You can confidently, authentically, and resolutely navigate the dating market as an older woman by actively confronting and eliminating these myths. Keep in mind that you have the authority to create your own story and look for relationships that are gratifying and meaningful despite conventional standards.

Myth: Older women are less tech-savvy and have trouble with contemporary dating techniques.

Overcoming Strategy: Demonstrate your aptitude for technology and agility. Demonstrate your comfort and expertise in navigating the online

Copyright ©

dating environment by becoming familiar with popular communication and dating platforms.

Misunderstanding: Older ladies simply want to settle down and get married.
Overcoming Strategy: Express your unique aspirations and objectives. Express your appreciation for the company and emotional connection, but also make clear that you are open to many types of relationships, including long-term partnerships, casual dating, and unconventional ones.

Myth: Older women are very judgmental or demanding.
Overcoming Strategy: Show that you have good communication skills by being courteous and empathic while expressing your wants and expectations. To encourage a positive and respectful environment in partnerships, emphasize your readiness to collaborate and make compromises.

Misconception: Older ladies don't like trying new things or going on adventures.
Overcoming Strategy: Express your love of learning and exploring yourself. Showcase your

willingness to try new things, whether it's taking up a new hobby, traveling, or taking part in intellectually interesting activities. Demonstrate that you like embracing life's chances and are open to new experiences.

Myth: Older women lack interest in or awareness of modern trends and popular culture.
Overcoming Strategy: Showcase your interest in current events, popular culture, and pertinent issues while being involved with the world around you. Break the myth that older women are out of touch by showcasing your ability to engage in meaningful conversation about a variety of topics.

You may defy stereotypes and approach dating with confidence and honesty by confronting these preconceptions and exhibiting your traits. Keep in mind that the strength of your character, your experiences, and the sincere relationships you create with others—rather than your age—determine your value and attractiveness.

Copyright ©

Overcoming Rejection Fear

Regardless of age, the fear of rejection is a frequent roadblock that may make dating difficult. It may stifle possibilities for connection, breed self-doubt, and discourage people from putting themselves out there. Recognizing that rejection is a normal part of the dating experience and shouldn't determine your self-worth is crucial. The following techniques will help you get over your fear of being rejected and approach dating with confidence:

Adopt a growth mindset and see rejection as a chance for development and education.

Recognize that it isn't an indictment of your character, but simply a mismatch in compatibility or circumstances. Reframing rejection as a step toward discovering a more suitable mate who values and respects you is possible by changing your attitude.

Practice Self-Compassion:

Copyright ©

Be gentle to yourself and understand that rejection is a part of the dating process for everyone. the empathy that rejection does not determine your value or invalidate your virtues, treat yourself with care and empathy. Keep in mind that you deserve love and connection and that setbacks are transient and necessary for progress.

Oppose Negative Self-Talk:

Be aware of negative self-talk that feeds your fear of being rejected and oppose it. Positive affirmations and reminders of your strengths and distinctive features should take the place of self-defeating remarks. Be in the company of positive, uplifting individuals who will assist you overcome any self-doubt.

Take Baby increments:

Begin by exposing yourself to possible rejection in tiny, achievable increments. This may include striking up a conversation, proposing a date, or participating in social events where you may meet new individuals. You may progressively expand your comfort zone and take on more difficult dating tasks as you gain self-assurance and resiliency.

Copyright ©

Change the emphasis from seeking external approval to seeking internal progress and contentment. Take part in activities that make you happy, boost your self-esteem, and let you follow your hobbies. By putting yourself first, you become less dependent on approval from others, which makes rejection less terrifying.

Keep in mind that rejection does not indicate how valuable a person you are. It only serves as a sign that you are not aligned or compatible with a certain person or circumstance. You may get over the fear of rejection and approach dating with a fresh feeling of confidence and authenticity by adopting a growth mindset, engaging in self-compassion, confronting negative self-talk, taking baby steps, and concentrating on personal improvement. Accept the adventure and have faith that the proper connections will materialize at the appropriate time.

Copyright ©

Chapter 3

Dating Protocol and Etiquette

To successfully navigate the difficulties of contemporary dating, dating etiquette is essential. It's crucial to understand the changing dynamics and expectations as an older woman entering the dating world. When it comes to dating etiquette, keep the following in mind:

Honesty and Clear Communication:
Establishing strong and lasting friendships requires open and honest communication. Early beginning, make sure to clarify your aims, goals, and limitations in detail. Honesty builds trust and lays the groundwork for a successful future partnership.Communication that is prompt and considerate is essential in the digital world we live in. Show consideration for the other person's time and interest by promptly responding to communications. It's polite to let someone know up

Copyright ©

front and honestly, if you can't fulfill their expectations or keep the relationship going.

Respect for Personal Limits and Consent:

Always respect personal limits and consent. Throughout the dating process, make sure you and your possible spouse feel secure and at ease. It's crucial to respect everyone's choices and not push them beyond their comfort zones.

Flexibility and Open-Mindedness:

Be receptive to fresh insights and other viewpoints. Nowadays, dating often means juggling a variety of lives, opinions, and tastes. Maintain an open mind and welcome the chance to learn and develop from various interactions as you approach each conversation.

Managing Rejection Well:

The dating process often involves rejection. Handle it with grace and respect whether someone shows interest or decides not to pursue a relationship. Refrain from taking offense or going on the defensive. Instead, keep your composure and advance with hope, certain that the proper link will materialize in due course.

Use social media responsibly:
In the digital era, dating is heavily influenced by social media. Utilize social networking sites carefully and responsibly, bearing in mind that how you present yourself online might affect how others see you. Respect privacy limits and refrain from prematurely disclosing too much personal information.

Keep in mind that proper dating etiquette focuses on encouraging courteous and thoughtful interactions rather than on following strict rules. You may confidently navigate the dating world and create genuine relationships by embracing open communication, upholding limits, being prompt and thankful, keeping adaptable and open-minded, taking rejection graciously, and utilizing social media with awareness.

Copyright ©

Presented as a dating metaphor for older women, Modern Rules

Present-Day Rules

Older women must be knowledgeable about the current dating norms in the ever-changing dating environment. Technology, shifting cultural standards, and the complexities of modern relationships all influence these principles. Here are some important contemporary guidelines for older women dating today:

Accept Online Dating:

Online dating is more common than ever and maybe a handy method to meet people. Accept the world of dating websites and apps, but be cautious and put your safety first. Spend some time developing an interesting and genuine profile that highlights your personality and hobbies.

Be Receptive to Various Relationship Dynamics: Different relationship dynamics are accepted in contemporary dating. Be open to trying out various relationships, whether they be short-term

Copyright ©

hookups, committed relationships, or unconventional pairings. Early on, be clear about your expectations for the relationship to guarantee compatibility and prevent misunderstandings.

Practice Active Consent:

In today's dating world, consent is crucial. Seek verbal or nonverbal clues from your spouse before moving on to physical intimacy to practice active consent. Respect their limits while being honest about your own. Keep in mind that consent should be passionate, continual, and freely given.

Accept Gender Equality:

Gender roles are more ambiguous and egalitarian in today's dating world. Accept the ideas of gender equality and dispel outdated prejudices. Whether it's starting talks, establishing plans, or delegating financial tasks, be proactive in expressing your opinions.

Use good digital manners:

Given the popularity of digital communication, good digital manners are essential. Pay attention to how you engage with others online and in text messages, on social media, and in dating applications. Abstain from ghosting, sending excessive or inappropriate messages, and other harmful online conduct.

Prioritize your safety while meeting new individuals by taking safety precautions. Initial encounters should be scheduled in public spaces. Let a friend or family member know what you're planning, and follow your gut. It's a good idea to do some research on a possible date to make sure they're real and safeguard your safety.

Maintain Individual Independence and Self-fulfillment:

Contemporary dating places a strong emphasis on the value of preserving personal independence and self-fulfillment. Alongside your dating efforts, focus on your hobbies, interests, and personal development. Prioritize your pleasure and well-being and avoid losing yourself in a relationship.

Copyright ©

Embrace Slow and Meaningful Interactions:

It's important to value slow and meaningful interactions in today's fast-paced digital environment. Spend time getting to know your possible spouse in-depth, have meaningful interactions with them, and create a foundation of emotional compatibility. The key is quality above quantity.

Be Open-Minded: Maintain an open mind and be prepared to confront your prejudices and preconceptions. embrace variety and many viewpoints to promote horizon-widening and personal development. Give yourself the chance to interact with people who may not suit your typical "type."

When navigating the current dating scene, follow your gut and trust your instincts. Never be afraid to take a step back and reevaluate a situation if anything seems weird or doesn't line up with your principles. You may follow your intuition to make decisions that are best for you.

Copyright ©

You may successfully navigate the dating scene as an older woman by being aware of and accepting these contemporary norms. Always be true to who you are, put your safety and well-being first, and go into every relationship with an open mind and a readiness to consider all the possibilities that the contemporary dating scene has to offer.

Guidelines for Older Women Dating:

Do not be ashamed of your age or your confidence.
Do work on developing self-acceptance and a good sense of yourself.
Accept your life's lessons and the knowledge they contain.
Do recognize and value the special dating chances that come with being an older lady.
Do talk openly and confidently about age-related issues.
Do dispel cultural myths and preconceptions regarding elderly ladies.

Copyright ©

Do embrace a development mentality and engage in self-compassion exercises to get over your fear of being rejected.

Do comprehend and abide by proper dating etiquette, which includes respecting limits and being explicit in communication.

Accept internet dating as a practical means of meeting possible companions.

When meeting new individuals, put personal safety first and take the appropriate safeguards.

Things to avoid while dating older women:

Never let your age define or restrict your value or attractiveness.

Don't feel pressured to live up to social standards or to compare yourself to younger ladies.

Don't allow social pressure or fear of being judged to stop you from making real relationships.

Avoid jumping into partnerships too quickly or accepting less than you deserve.

Don't allow heartbreaks or unpleasant memories from the past to influence how you date now and in the future.

Copyright ©

Don't base your sense of value simply on the opinions of others.
In partnerships, don't be scared to voice your needs, wants, and limits.
Don't allow self-doubt or negative self-talk to interfere with your dating life.
Do not undervalue the significance of dating and personal development.
Keep your independence and uniqueness, and avoid losing yourself in a relationship.

Don't undervalue the value of flexibility and an open mind. Be prepared to stretch yourself and accept new viewpoints, experiences, and interpersonal patterns. A relationship shouldn't be shaped by inflexible expectations or preconceived beliefs about how it should develop based on age or social expectations. Keep an open mind to new opportunities, and permit yourself to be surprised by the connections you create.
You may negotiate the dating scene as an older woman with assurance, honesty, and a feeling of strength by adhering to these dos and don'ts. Keep in mind to value your individuality, put self-care and personal development first, and see every dating

Copyright ©

encounter as a chance for connection, development, and joy.

Rules for dating older women

For older women hoping to make new friends and even discover a love companion, dating can be an exciting and rewarding experience. There are some conventions and principles that may assist you navigate the process, just like with any sort of dating. These procedures may boost the self-assurance of older ladies and guarantee a great dating experience. Let's look at 30 rules for dating older ladies.

Embrace your self-assurance:
Older women provide a lot of insight and life experience. When dating, embrace your self-assurance and highlight your talents.

An example would be to participate in meaningful talks that showcase your expertise and experiences while on a date by telling amusing anecdotes from your life.

Copyright ©

Be open-minded:
When dating, have an open mind and be prepared to consider individuals from varied backgrounds, ages, and hobbies.

As an example, think about going on dates with people who could have different interests or viewpoints. This could result in interesting and rewarding encounters.

Recognize the qualities you're seeking in a mate and establish reasonable expectations.
You may prevent disappointment and make wiser dating decisions as a result.

Example: If you're looking for a long-term partner, concentrate on those that show compatibility and shared values.

Make communication a priority since it's essential to every connection
Openly and honestly express your needs, wants, and ideas.

For instance, to guarantee compatibility and mutual understanding early in the dating process, communicate your expectations, limits, and aspirations.

Copyright ©

Adopt current technology:
To increase your dating pool and communicate with possible companions, use online dating platforms and applications.

Use technology to connect with people who share your interests and traits, for instance, by creating a dating profile that promotes such things.

Enjoy the journey:
Engage in dating as a self-discovery adventure and relish the opportunity to meet new individuals.

Example: Enjoy the thrill of getting to know someone and value the chances for personal development that dating may provide.

Look after yourself:
To feel your best and exude confidence, prioritize taking care of yourself and lead a healthy lifestyle.

Example : Do things that make you happy, exercise often, eat well-balanced meals, and prioritize getting enough sleep.

Keep your independence and go on pursuing your interests and objectives outside of the relationship.

Copyright ©

Example: To guarantee a balanced and enjoyable existence, schedule social events with friends, pursue hobbies, and work on one's personal development.

Be open to exploring new things and accept spontaneity when it comes to your dating endeavors. For instance, propose going on an impromptu date or recommend trying a novel restaurant or activity together.

Exercise patience;
creating a lasting bond takes time. Be patient and let the connections grow.
For instance, don't hurry into choices and take the time to get to know your date well before doing so.

Focus on compatibility:
To build a solid connection, look for individuals who share your beliefs, hobbies, and long-term objectives.
Example: To maximize the probability of a good relationship, look for people who have matching ideals and lifestyles.

Keep a sense of humor:

Copyright ©

Laughter may deepen bonds and provide unforgettable experiences. Keep a sense of humor and take pleasure in fun times.

Example: To create a lively and engaging ambiance, share humorous stories, and jokes, or engage in lighthearted conversation with your date.

Reflect on yourself often to make sure you're making good dating decisions by evaluating your own needs, desires, and limits.

Take some time to think back on your dating experiences, draw lessons from them, and make any required changes to your approach moving forward.

Be considerate:

Respectfully treat your date and anticipate receiving it in return. Establish sound limits and deal with any issues forcefully.

Observe your date's time, for instance.

As an example, be considerate of your date's schedule and arrive on time for planned excursions.

Copyright ©

Expect your date to respect your schedule and obligations in the same manner.

When it comes to dating, follow your instincts and pay attention to your feelings. Consider taking the appropriate precautions to protect yourself if anything doesn't seem right.
As an example, follow your instincts when you sense something is amiss or you are uneasy, and voice your concerns or leave the situation immediately.

Keep in mind that these dating rules are just intended to be used as a broad guideline. Feel free to modify them to fit your tastes and situation because every person and relationship is unique. Love your dates!

Respect your limits, and let your date know what they are straightforwardly and concisely.
Respect your date's limits in the same way.

Copyright ©

For instance, if you're uncomfortable with physical touch on a first date, make sure to politely state your limits and demand that they be upheld.

Don't compare too much:
Concentrate on the person in front of you rather than continually drawing comparisons to previous partners or relationships.

Give your date a chance to succeed on their terms and refrain from drawing frequent comparisons that can prevent you from developing a genuine relationship.

Promote well-being and self-care:
Maintain a focus on your health during the dating process. Take pauses when necessary, practice self-care, and prioritize your emotional and physical well-being.

For instance, if you're experiencing emotional exhaustion or overload during dating, take a break, indulge in reviving activities, and then resume dating when you're ready.

Appreciate your freedom:
As an older woman, embrace and appreciate your independence. Make it clear to your date that you

respect your independence and are at ease with who you are.

Example: To show your independence and motivate your date, tell tales about your successes, adventures, or individual accomplishments.

Practice gratitude:

Even if your dating encounters don't result in long-term relationships, be grateful for the good parts of them. You may keep a happy view and bring more optimism into your life by adopting this mentality.

Even if a date doesn't work out, take a minute to appreciate the good times and lessons you learned from it.

Demonstrate empathy and understanding by being considerate of your date's experiences, viewpoints, and feelings. This promotes friendship and respect for one another.

As an example, when your date discusses personal struggles or tales, validate their emotions and demonstrate empathy by providing support and understanding.

Be receptive to friendship:

Copyright ©

While seeking a love relationship, be receptive to forming sincere friendships as well. Even if not every date may result in a romantic partnership, it is still possible to make worthwhile friendships.

For instance, rather than cutting off a relationship suddenly if the love chemistry isn't there but you still like being with the other person, think about fostering a friendship.

Accept vulnerability:

Permit yourself to be open and honest with your date. This fosters a climate of trust and strengthens relationships.

Give the following example to your date to help them get to know the real you and develop a stronger sense of connection.

Be nice and sympathetic to yourself during the dating process by practicing self-compassion.

You should treat yourself with the same compassion and consideration that you would show a dear friend.

Example: Remind yourself that rejection or a date that doesn't go as planned is common, and try not to be too hard on yourself.

Copyright ©

Continually be yourself:

Keep your integrity and be faithful to your goals, interests, and values. Don't let a relationship cause you to sacrifice your fundamental self.

Be honest about your interests, pastimes, and viewpoints, for instance. To win your date's favor, avoid pretending to be someone you're not.

Engage in active self-reflection by regularly reflecting on your dating experiences to see trends or potential development opportunities. Self-awareness may help us make wiser decisions and more satisfying interactions.

To get insight into yourself and your dating preferences, spend some time reflecting in a diary or during meditation on your dating experiences. Pay attention to your emotions, ideas, and responses.

Copyright ©

Develop a supporting network:
Surround yourself with a network of friends and family members who can provide advice, inspiration, and a listening ear while you navigate the dating world.
Example: Consult reliable friends or family members who can provide insightful advice and support on dating, or talk to them about your dating experiences.

Remember that dating is a chance to meet new people and connect with them, but it's also crucial to put your happiness and well-being first. Adapt these guidelines to your situation and enjoy the opportunity to meet new individuals. I wish you luck!

Typical blunders on a first date

For older women who may be reentering the dating scene or looking for new relationships, first dates may be particularly nerve-wracking. It's crucial to be aware of typical blunders and take preventative measures to avoid them if you want to guarantee a

Copyright ©

successful and pleasurable first date. Discover the top first-date blunders to avoid in this article.

Error:

Focusing too much on the past might make things uncomfortable and take the attention away from the present.

Preventive advice: Keep the talk light and on-topic. Spend less time talking about your ex and more time getting to know your date.

Neglecting personal grooming:

Neglecting personal grooming might come off as uninterested or lazy.

Prevention: Give personal cleanliness, suitable dress, grooming routines, and grooming a high priority. Being well-groomed demonstrates self-respect and conveys your importance to the date.

Constantly checking your phone while on a date is a bad idea since it shows that you're uninterested and unengaged.

To prevent distractions, keep your phone out of sight or in quiet mode. Pay close attention to your date and show that you are interested in what they have to say.

Copyright ©

Too critical behavior:
Being too critical or judgemental might exacerbate a good relationship.
Prevention: Keep an open mind, be curious, and be accepting of the date. Instead of focusing on faults, discover points of agreement and explore mutual interests.

Mistake:
Not listening attentively might result in misunderstandings and lost possibilities for deeper relationships.
Practice active listening by keeping eye contact, nodding, and asking pertinent follow-up questions as a preventative measure. To encourage meaningful conversation, show real interest in what your date is saying.

Being too cautious:
A true relationship can't grow if one is unduly on guard and walled off.
Prevention: Be willing to show vulnerability and offer relevant personal anecdotes and experiences. An openness and genuineness level are necessary to develop trust.

Copyright ©

Disclosing too much private information

On a first date, divulging too much personal information may be overwhelming and unsettling.

Prevention: Strike a balance between keeping private and sharing. Share just enough to establish a rapport, but hold off on revealing too much sensitive or profoundly personal information.

Discussing contentious or delicate subjects:

Discussions on delicate or contentious subjects might result in arguments and discomfort.

Preventive advice: Have lighthearted, upbeat talks. Steer clear of subjects like politics, religion, or contentious matters that can cause conflict. Look for themes that will provide for entertaining discussion and shared interests.

Being too tense or self-conscious:

Genuine relationships might be hampered if you let anxiety or self-consciousness overpower your personality.

Prevention: Breathe deeply, tell yourself to unwind, and pay attention to the here and now. Accept who you are and let your individuality come through.

In control of the conversation:

Talking too much and not letting your date speak out might be uncomfortable and inhibit open dialogue.

Prevention: Engage in active listening and give your date enough time to express their ideas and personal narratives. Talk back and forth in a way that encourages equal involvement.

Ignoring one's boundaries:

Negative dates may result from disregarding personal boundaries and making your date feel uncomfortable.

Prevention: Be aware of your personal space, refrain from making invasive inquiries, and respect your date's level of comfort. By establishing and observing your limits, you may provide a respectful and secure atmosphere for others.

Rush toward intimacy:

Moving too early or forcing physical closeness on your date might lead to pain and sabotage the chance for a deep relationship.

Prevention: Spend some time building emotional and trusting closeness before going on to physical intimacy. Respect the limits of your date and allow the connection to develop organically.

Complaining or acting negatively:
Mistake: Complaining or acting negatively all the time might be annoying and make the date less enjoyable.
Prevention: Keep a cheerful and upbeat attitude. Engage in discussions that are uplifting and inspiring and concentrate on the good parts of your life. Make space for fun interactions and lighthearted comedy.

Being very future-oriented
Mistake: Bringing too many expectations and plans for the future on a date might make you feel stressed and under pressure.
Prevention: Enjoy getting to know your date and be in the moment. Don't talk about long-term goals or make predictions. Let the bond develop spontaneously.

Absence of appreciation or thanks

Copyright ©

It might be detrimental to the possibility of continued connection to fail to show thanks or appreciation for the date.

Prevention: Authentically expresses your gratitude for your date's time, effort, and company. Thank everyone for the fun times and interesting talks.

Being too concerned about appearance:

Overemphasizing physical looks might take the focus off of compatibility and real connection.

Prevention: Put more emphasis on getting to know your date's personality, beliefs, and interests rather than on how they seem physically. Consider compatibility in addition to obvious characteristics.

Not requesting follow-up inquiries:

Skipping the follow-up inquiries might come off as uninterested and prevent fruitful interaction.

To avoid this, ask meaningful follow-up questions that are based on your date's replies. This displays active participation and promotes a closer bond.

Copyright ©

Ignoring intuition or red flags:

Neglecting intuition or warning signs may result in partnerships that are potentially harmful or incompatible.

Prevention: Trust your gut and be aware of any warning signals or red flags that come up throughout the date. Put your safety and well-being first by speaking about any worries you may have and acting appropriately.

Expectations that are too high for the date:

Making the mistake of having too high of expectations for the first date might result in disappointment and unneeded stress.

Prevention: Go on the first date with an open mind and no expectations in mind. Be open to several outcomes and let the relationship develop spontaneously.

Being very future-oriented:

Talking too much about your date's aspirations for the future might put a strain on the relationship and make it harder to appreciate the moment as it is.

Prevention: Be mindful of your surroundings and concentrate on getting to know your date better.

Copyright ©

Avoid making assumptions about the future of the relationship or talking excessively about future obligations. Let events develop spontaneously.

Omitting to express gratitude

Mistake: It might come off as unappreciative or uninterested if you forget to thank your date for their efforts and company.

Take the time to express your appreciation for your date's time, considerate actions, and the experiences you two have experienced. Making your date feel appreciated may be accomplished by saying thanks or offering a compliment.

Being very self-centered:

Negative impressions might be created when you dominate the discussion and just discuss yourself while not demonstrating any interest in your date's life.

Prevention: Attempt to participate in a fair dialogue and engage in active listening. Be genuinely curious about your date's life, beliefs, and interests. Making an effort to connect with them can help you come off as sincere.

Copyright ©

Bringing up delicate or contentious subjects

Talking about sensitive or contentious topics, such as politics or previous traumas, on a first date may lead to tension and discomfort.

Prevention: Talk in an upbeat and lighthearted manner. Avoid potentially polarizing subjects and concentrate on common passions, pastimes, or fun activities. Set a comfortable and calm mood for the two of you.

Hastily defining or labeling the relationship:

Early labeling or relationship definition might put undue strain on the relationship and stifle natural development.

Prevention: Let the connection develop naturally. Avoid expecting commitment too soon or defining the relationship too quickly. Without having too many expectations on the first date, enjoy getting to know each other.

You may improve the quality of your first dates and raise the possibility of developing lasting relationships by being aware of these extra faults and taking proactive measures to avoid them.

Copyright ©

Always remember to go on dates with an open mind, genuine interest, and readiness to enjoy the process of getting to know someone.

Keep in mind that dating is a learning process and that errors will inevitably be made. You may improve your chances of having a successful and happy first date by being thoughtful, and self-aware, and implementing these preventative actions. Enjoy the procedure and seize the chance to meet new people!

Copyright ©

Copyright ©

Chapter: 4

Setting Priorities and Goals for Your Dating Life

This chapter will discuss how crucial it is for older women to establish their dating objectives and aspirations. Clarifying what you want from a partner will not only help you navigate the dating process but will also give you the ability to make decisions that are consistent with your goals and beliefs.

Considering Your Relationship Needs and Aspirations:
Consider your requirements and desires in a relationship as a starting point. Think about the traits and principles you want in a spouse. Are you looking for a long-term relationship, emotional connection, or companionship? Be honest with yourself about your expectations and determine what you genuinely want in a relationship.

Copyright ©

Choosing Your Must-Haves and Deal-Breakers:

Determining your deal-breakers and must-haves is equally important. These are the qualities you must have in a partner or those you just cannot tolerate. Shared ideals, compatibility, or particular lifestyle preferences may be examples of this. Knowing your deal-breakers will enable you to screen possible mates and will help you save time and effort when dating.

Setting Reasonable Goals and Respecting Your Boundaries

A successful dating experience depends on having reasonable expectations. Recognize that relationships need work and compromise and that perfection is unattainable. Additionally, set up limits that are in line with your beliefs and level of comfort. Prioritize your mental health and let prospective partners know about your limits.

Matching Dating Objectives to Life Priorities

Think about how your dating objectives fit with your top priorities in life. You could have successful work, responsibilities to your family, or personal

Copyright ©

interests as an older lady. Establish a balance that seems good for you between dating and your overall life goal. Don't forget that maintaining a full life outside of romantic relationships should be a top priority.

Embracing Openness and Flexibility

Determining your dating objectives is crucial, but you should also be open to new opportunities and surprising connections. The most satisfying partnerships may sometimes arise in unexpected locations. Keep an open mind and be prepared to investigate connections that may not fit your first criterion.

Honoring Personal Evolution and Growth

Finally, keep in mind that your dating objectives and priorities could change over time. Your wants and desires may alter as you mature and gain greater self-awareness. Accept your personal development and let your dating life change as a result. Stay loyal to who you are and be prepared to reevaluate your objectives as required.

Copyright ©

You empower yourself to make deliberate decisions in your love life by setting dating objectives and goals. Spend some time introspecting, establishing limits, and integrating your dating objectives with your aims. This clarity will boost your self-assurance and eventually result in more satisfying interactions for you as an older lady.

Deciding what you truly want and refusing to accept anything less

It's essential to know what you genuinely want in a relationship and have the confidence to not settle for anything less while looking for love. The advice in this chapter will help you identify your preferences, establish reasonable expectations, and select a partner who shares your goals and beliefs.

Knowing Your Inner Motives:
Start by looking deep inside yourself to discover what it is about relationships that genuinely fulfill you. Spend some time reflecting on your

requirements, preferences, and objectives. Think about the traits, principles, and aspects of your lifestyle that are significant to you. This self-awareness will guide you as you navigate the dating world.

Acknowledging Your Value and Self-Respect

Accept and believe in your value. You deserve to be in a relationship that fulfills you and makes you happy. By being aware of your worth and upholding your dignity, you may avoid settling for less than you deserve. You will attract companions who value and appreciate you if you respect your self-worth.

Making a List of Your Non-Negotiables

Determine your non-negotiables or the fundamental principles and characteristics you look for in a spouse. You must not compromise on these factors since they represent your core requirements for a suitable and satisfying relationship. Be explicit about the qualities you want and cannot have in a mate. You may make educated choices and prevent settling for someone who doesn't fulfill your requirements by being aware of your non-negotiables.

Copyright ©

Identification of Red Flags and Deal-Breakers:

Be watchful for warning signs and deal-breakers in prospective relationships. These are red flags or actions that conflict with your ideals or make you feel uneasy. Trust your gut and pay attention to any warning signals; they may point to future difficulties or incompatibility. Have the bravery to leave a situation if required when it is not in line with your needs.

Setting Limits and Making Your Needs Clear:

Set and maintain appropriate limits during dating. Potential partners should be made aware of your requirements, expectations, and limitations. Don't be scared to stand up for yourself in a relationship and make an effort to get what you want. Setting and upholding limits ensures that your needs are addressed and that you are respected. Stay committed to your limits and assertively state them to avoid settling for less.

Having endurance and patience

Copyright ©

It could take some time and patience to find someone who shares your goals in a mate. Recognize that the road to a happy relationship might be filled with ups and downs. Even in the face of difficulties or brief loneliness, maintain your resolve to never accept less. You will be helped in your quest to discover a suitable and happy relationship by having patience and resilience.

Increasing Your Choices and Openness

It is necessary to remain open to new ideas while maintaining clear standards and limitations. The ideal spouse may sometimes arrive in unique packaging or exhibit unanticipated traits. Keep your alternatives open and your mind open while adhering to your primary aspirations and principles.

Getting Support and Direction:

Don't be afraid to ask dependable family members, friends, or experts for advice and assistance. Talk to them about your aspirations, worries, and past experiences. They may provide insightful opinions, guidance, and assistance to help you navigate the dating world and make wise choices.

Copyright ©

You may empower yourself to forge a satisfying and suitable connection by being honest with yourself about what you want in a relationship and having the confidence to not settle for less. Accept your value, list your absolutes, and maintain sound limits. In your quest for a connection that matches your values, trust your intuition, practice patience, and persevere.

Reevaluating Relationship Objectives and Keeping Partnership and Independence in Check

It's crucial to reevaluate your relationship objectives as an older woman to make sure they suit your current stage of life and wants. Here are some important factors to remember:

Take the time to consider your priorities and what you want in a relationship at this point in your life. Are you looking for company, emotional support, or hobbies and interests in common? Making your priorities clear will enable you to decide on the kinds of relationships you wish to pursue.

Embrace Emotional Compatibility:
Check to see whether a possible spouse and you have a strong emotional connection. For a relationship to be meaningful and long-lasting, there must be shared values, efficient communication, and a strong emotional connection. Put emotional closeness first, and look for a mate who can satisfy your emotional demands.

Be Flexible and Realistic:
Be flexible and truthful about the realities of dating as you become older. Recognize that it can be difficult to locate a spouse who checks off every item on your list. Find someone who shares your basic beliefs, treats you with respect, and encourages your personal development instead.

Take into account various relationship philosophies:
Older women may have various relationship aims and inclinations. While some may choose more informal or unconventional arrangements, others

Copyright ©

could be looking for a long-term, committed relationship. There is no one-size-fits-all strategy for relationships, so experiment with many relationship styles to see which one suits you the best.

Openness to Intergenerational connections:

Be open to the idea of connections across generations, even when there is a big age gap. These connections may open doors to new viewpoints, learning opportunities, and experiences. However, make sure that both parties are in agreement concerning their expectations and compatibility over the long run.

Navigating Blended Families:

If you have children or grandkids, think about how your family dynamics may be affected by a new partnership. It takes time, tolerance, and respect for limits to integrate a new spouse into your family. Look for a partner who is willing to handle the challenges of blended families and who appreciates and understands your position as a parent or grandmother.

Copyright ©

Prioritize your Development:
While looking for a satisfying relationship is crucial, give your development priority. Pay attention to the interests and activities that make you happy, improve your well-being, and add to your overall sense of contentment. Future relationships will only benefit from having a positive, balanced view of yourself.

Take Your Time:
Don't feel compelled to settle or hasten the beginning of a relationship. Spend some time getting to know prospective mates at a pace that seems natural to you. Trust your instincts and judgment along the way as the connection develops gradually.

Embrace Independence:
For older women in relationships, it's essential to strike a balance between independence and collaboration. Make careful to keep your autonomy, individuality, and personal interests intact. Your independence should be supported and increased, not reduced, in a good relationship.

Copyright ©

Balance of Independence and Partnership

Finding the right mix of independence and cooperation as an older woman entering the dating scene is crucial for a strong and happy relationship. Following are some tips to help you strike this balance:

Define limits: From the start of a partnership, set up clear limits. Be clear about your wants, boundaries, and me-time. Your limits will be respected, and a supportive spouse will support your independence.

Maintain Your Interests: Keep up with your interests and pastimes. Keeping a good balance between independence and collaboration requires keeping a feeling of self and participating in things that make you happy and fulfilled. Don't abandon your interests or passions just because you are in a relationship. Encourage your spouse to explore their hobbies so that both of you may continue to be unique and develop personally.

Copyright ©

Open communication is essential for achieving a healthy balance between independence and collaboration.

Your spouse should understand your needs and wants, and you should urge them to do the same. Find a happy medium where you can both feel valued and encouraged in your endeavors while still preserving your relationship.

Foster interdependence:

Aim for a relationship where both partners actively support and rely on one other while yet maintaining their freedom. Realize that joining a partnership does not entail giving up your independence. By combining your skills, assuming one another's tasks, and encouraging one another's professional and personal development, embrace interdependence.

Prioritize Quality Time Together:

While maintaining your independence is vital, making time for your partnership is just as critical. Make a deliberate effort to develop emotional connections, share meaningful experiences, and have meaningful discussions. Finding the ideal balance between "me" and "we" time is necessary to maintain both independence and relationship.

Copyright ©

A healthy relationship is built on the principles of trust and respect. Have faith that your spouse values and encourages your independence. Respect and trust should also be shown for your partner's demand for independence. You may both work for your separate objectives while still having a solid foundation of trust in your partnership.

Seek Emotional Support:

Having emotional support in your relationship is crucial. As you manage your ambitions, rely on your spouse for support, understanding, and encouragement. Provide your spouse with the same degree of emotional support. While recognizing and respecting each other's individuality, this support strengthens the feeling of partnership.

Maintain Healthy Boundaries:

Maintaining healthy boundaries within the partnership is just as critical as supporting each other's independence. Set boundaries for conduct or acts that could invade your personal space or threaten your independence. Healthy boundaries make sure that both parties in a relationship feel respected and appreciated.

Copyright ©

The balance between independence and collaboration requires continual reflection and adjustment. Consider your requirements often and reevaluate the nature of your connection. Be willing to make changes and have open discussions about keeping a good balance. Finding balance in your relationship requires adaptation and flexibility.

Celebrate Your Individual and Collective Successes:

Recognize and honor your individual and collective successes. Recognize one other's successes and assist one another in achieving their objectives. This victory celebration serves as more proof that you may achieve personal achievement while cultivating a solid, dependable relationship.

You may achieve a healthy balance between independence and collaboration in your dating life as an older woman by reevaluating your relationship objectives, embracing independence, cultivating interdependence, and maintaining open communication. Always keep in mind that attaining the ideal balance is specific to each relationship and

Copyright ©

requires ongoing self-evaluation, communication, and mutual support.

Establishing limits and expectations

For an older woman to continue to have a positive and rewarding dating experience, clear limits are essential. When setting personal limits, keep the following in mind:

Consider Your Requirements:

Give some thought to your relationship priorities and individual requirements. Recognize the things that make you feel respected, safe, and at ease. Decide which limits are most essential to you, whether they be time, emotional, or physical.

Be Clear About Your Limits:

Let prospective partners know exactly what your limits are. Be forceful and clear about your expectations from the start of the relationship. This helps provide the groundwork for mutual understanding and trust by ensuring that both parties are aware of and respect each other's boundaries.

Be Firm and Consistent: After you've set your limits, maintain them with firmness and

Copyright ©

consistency. Don't give in to pressure to please others or avoid confrontation by compromising your limits. Your spouse should respect your limits since they are crucial to your mental health.

Trust Your Gut:

When it comes to establishing limits, trust your gut. It's crucial to follow your gut feeling if something doesn't seem right or line up with your ideals. You may follow your gut instinct when deciding what limits are required to sustain a positive and respectful relationship.

Saying no when something is against your own beliefs or comfort zone is a crucial part of setting boundaries. Practice being aggressive and expressing your boundaries with assurance. Keep in mind that exercising self-care and respect for oneself by saying no is not being selfish.

Boundaries may change as you navigate various relationships and life events, so adjust them as necessary. Be willing to modify your boundaries as needed to accommodate the particular dynamics of each relationship and the personal development you go through.

Copyright ©

Managing Expectations

To prevent disappointments and foster stronger relationships, expectations management is crucial. The following advice can help you control your expectations during dating:

Be Realistic:

Set reasonable goals for yourself in terms of dating and relationships. Recognize that no one is perfect and that for a relationship to work, both sides must be willing to compromise and show empathy. Avoid having unattainable expectations since they might leave you feeling let down all the time.

Prioritize Emotional Connection and Compatibility:

Prioritize emotional connection and compatibility instead of concentrating just on exterior qualities like beauty or monetary assets. To have a meaningful connection, look for individuals that share your beliefs, ambitions, and interests.

Copyright ©

Transparent communication is essential for controlling expectations. Regarding your needs, wants, and ambitions, be forthright and honest. Early on, talk about your expectations with your partner to make sure you're on the same page and are aware of each other's expectations for the relationship.

Relationships are dynamic, therefore it's important to be flexible. Be ready to change course and make concessions if needed. Recognize that you and your spouse could have different wants and expectations and that finding a middle ground involves flexibility and openness.

Spend some time developing trust since it takes time. Avoid making hasty commitments or expecting complete trust right away. Spend the time and space necessary to build a solid foundation of trust and emotional connection with your spouse.

Prioritize Effective Communication:

By promoting understanding and clarity, effective communication helps manage expectations. Express your wants and worries, engage in active listening, and urge your spouse to do the same. It is possible to avoid misunderstandings and foster healthy

Copyright ©

relationship dynamics by being open and honest with one another.

Be Self-Aware:
Spend some time reflecting on your expectations and relational habits. Recognize any prejudices or baggage from the past that may have an impact on your aspirations. You may approach dating with a clearer perspective and make better decisions when it comes to controlling and establishing your expectations if you are self-aware.

Accept the Journey:
Dating is an exploration and learning process. Accept the process and have an open mind to new opportunities and experiences. Don't put too much pressure on yourself to locate the ideal spouse or to move too quickly. Enjoy the process of getting to know others better by letting connections develop spontaneously.

Practice Self-Compassion:
As you negotiate the dating scene, be nice and sympathetic to yourself. Understanding that not every relationship will succeed is acceptable. Don't criticize or blame yourself if things don't turn out the

Copyright ©

way you planned. Throughout the dating process, be kind, compassionate, and patient with yourself.

Seek Alignment, Not Perfection:

Pay attention to achieving alignment rather than pursuing perfection in a partner or relationship. Look for someone who is in line with your long-term objectives, your basic beliefs, and your personal development. It is more important to build a strong foundation based on shared values and respect for one another than to strive for some elusive notion of perfection.

You may handle the dating scene with self-assurance and confidence by establishing personal boundaries and controlling your expectations. Always be honest with communication, believe in your gut, and put your emotional health first. You can develop better and more satisfying relationships with prospective partners by doing this.

Copyright ©

Copyright ©

Chapter: 5

Effective Listening and Empathy

Forging lasting ties in the dating world, effective communication is crucial. To improve your communication abilities as an older woman, consider the following fundamental ideas:

Give your spouse your undivided attention as you engage in active listening. Maintain eye contact, show real interest in what they are saying, and refrain from interrupting. Avoid distractions that can impair successful communication and concentrate on comprehending their point of view.

By placing yourself in your partner's shoes, you may develop empathy. Make an effort to comprehend their feelings, experiences, and viewpoint. Empathy promotes understanding and affirmation in your relationships and enables deeper connections.

Non-Verbal indicators: Pay attention to non-verbal indicators including tone of voice, body language, and facial expressions. These signs might provide you with more information about your partner's feelings and intentions. Be aware of your nonverbal cues and make sure they support the message you want to convey.

Practice reflective listening by summarizing or paraphrasing what your companion has said. By using this strategy, you may show that you are participating in the dialogue and you are validating their sentiments and experiences. It also aids in removing any confusion that could exist.

By embracing and recognizing your partner's sentiments without passing judgment, you are validating their emotions and experiences. Even if you don't entirely agree with their viewpoint, show support and understanding. A secure and open environment for communication is created when their feelings are validated.

Copyright ©

Assertive Communication Techniques

The secret to clearly and respectfully expressing your needs, limits, and desires is assertive communication. The following are some methods to improve forceful communication:

Use "I" sentences to communicate your demands and emotions without coming off as accusing. Saying "You always ignore me," for instance, is preferable to "I feel hurt when I don't receive your attention."

Expressing limits:
Make sure to make your expectations and limits clear. Express what in a relationship you find acceptable and unacceptable with firmness and candor. This fosters respect and understanding between parties.

Use the active voice to speak in a self-assured and authoritative manner. Avoid using language that is apologetic or passive since it will lessen the impact of your message. Speak clearly and with conviction.

Self-reflection is a good habit to get into. Consider your needs, beliefs, and desires before entering into crucial interactions. You may express yourself truthfully and forcefully thanks to this self-reflection without sacrificing your sense of self.

Use Powerful Body Language:
When communicating, be aware of your body language. Keep a straight stance, create suitable eye contact, and use movements that help to convey your message. Your speech might have a greater effect if you use assertive body language.

Navigating Difficult Conversations

In every relationship, difficult topics will always arise. Here's how to steer clear of them:

Pick a time and location that are ideal for the talk, assuring seclusion and reducing outside noise. This fosters an atmosphere that is favorable for direct and honest communication.

Keep your emotions under control during challenging interactions by being collected and calm. Breathe deeply, use restraint, and strive to maintain a cool and serene attitude. This keeps the conversation civil and fruitful.

Active Listening:

Pay attention to your partner's point of view while avoiding interruptions and showing off. Demonstrate compassion and make an effort to comprehend their viewpoint. This encourages a dialogue that is more beneficial and cooperative.

Use "I" Statements: Avoid blaming or criticizing your spouse and instead concentrate on expressing your thoughts and emotions. The use of "I" comments may keep the discussion from devolving into a debate and promote a more cooperative and sympathetic method of problem-solving.

Copyright ©

Asking clarifying questions can help you better grasp your partner's emotions, ideas, and motives. Avoid assuming or drawing hasty judgments. This indicates your ability to pay attention and your respect for their viewpoint.

Describe Yourself Clearly:

Use assertive communication skills to state your requirements and concerns clearly and concisely. To further explain your views and add perspective, use concrete examples. Deliver your message politely yet firmly.

Instead of lingering on the issue, put your attention on potential solutions and areas of agreement. Work together to generate ideas and find a solution to the current problem with your partner.

Compromise in action:

Be willing to develop solutions that satisfy both your demands and those of your spouse. Recognize that there are several "correct" solutions to every argument since relationships call for compromise. Finding common ground may improve your relationship and promote mutual understanding.

Take Breaks if Necessary:

It's OK to take breaks if emotions grow too intense or the discussion turns tense. Take a little break to collect your thoughts, relax, and recover composure. Resuming the talk after clearing your head might result in a more fruitful discussion.

After a challenging talk, check in with your spouse to see whether any agreements or settlements have been carried through. Return to the subject often to evaluate your progress and, if necessary, make changes. Healthy partnerships need constant discussion and open communication.

As an older woman, you may create stronger and more fulfilling relationships by developing your communication abilities, working on being more asscrtive and handling challenging talks with understanding and respect. Stronger understanding, increased trust, and successful communication all help your relationships as a whole.

Copyright ©

How to interact with a prospective partner when out on a first date

On a first date, it's critical to find a balance between being authentic, getting to know the other person, and establishing a welcoming and stimulating environment. Following are some suggestions on what to say and what not to say, along with instances of useful conversation:

Authenticity & Sincerity

DO: Express your sincere passions, hobbies, and interests.
I've always been captivated by photography and like documenting special moments, for instance. Do you have any passions or hobbies?

AVOID: Pretending to be someone you're not in an attempt to impress.

Copyright ©

I like extreme sports, for instance. Two times, I've scaled Mount Everest. (if you haven't done it)

Open-ended inquiries:

DO: Encourage the other individual to disclose more about themselves by asking open-ended questions.
Why did you decide to pursue a profession in marketing, for instance? More about your travels, please.

AVOID: Getting too personal or interfering with others.
As an example, "So, how much money do you make?"

Engage in Active Listening and Interest:

DO: Actively listen to what they have to say and reply with genuine interest.
"That's fascinating!" for instance. I understand why you are so devoted to your profession. What do you enjoy best about it?

AVOID dominating or interfering with the discourse.

Copyright ©

"Enough about you," for instance. Let me share with you some of my incredible achievements.

Positive Experiences and Stories to Share

DO: Talk about happy occasions or tales that illustrate your character and principles.
Example: "My recent volunteer experience at a nearby animal shelter was fulfilling. Do you like helping the community out?

AVOID: Over Complaining or dwelling on the bad things that have happened.
For instance: "Dating has been awful recently. Simply said, none of the individuals I encounter are worth my attention.

Humorousness and Light-Heartedness

DO: Use humor to make the environment fun and jovial.
Example: "I just went to a cooking class, and when I got home my kitchen looked like a battle zone. At least no one, though, contracted food poisoning.

Copyright ©

Avoid using sarcasm or harsh humor that might be misconstrued or embarrass the other person.
"You're not like most women I meet," for instance. You do seem to be clever.

Identical Interests:

DO: Find areas of agreement and express your passion for like-minded pursuits.
I've heard you like trekking, for instance. I also like hiking new paths. Have you had a favorite place to hike?

Avoid acting as if you have hobbies that you don't to impress the other person.
For instance: "Oh, I love classical music a lot. even have a violin." (when you lack expertise or understanding in that field)

Demonstrate curiosity and mutual learning:

DO: Show interest in and want to learn from the other person.
For instance: "I've never tried surfing. How did you get involved? Any advice for a novice like me?

Copyright ©

AVOID: Taking control of the discussion or making it seem like an interrogation.
Tell me anything about your prior relationships, for instance.

Stay Upbeat and Steer Clear of Controversial Subjects:

DO: Concentrate on upbeat and humorous subjects that foster a nice mood.
Example: "What are your preferred vacation spots? I like learning about other cultures and tasting new foods.

AVOID: Bringing up delicate or divisive subjects that can cause conflict or distress.
For instance, "Let's discuss both political and religious beliefs.

Praise & Appreciation:

DO: Compliment the other person sincerely and show your thanks.
I must add that you have an outstanding sense of style. You have a keen sense of style.

Copyright ©

AVOID: Offering phony or too general praises.
Example: "You look nice" (without any more information or individualized phrasing).

Share Your Future Goals:

DO: Express your goals and aspirations by sharing your objectives and aspirations.
Example: "In the coming years, I want to start my own business and travel more. Hello, how are you? What goals do you intend to accomplish for the future?

AVOID: Overcrowding the conversation with details or coming across as overly focused on one's successes.
Example: "I want to be a millionaire and own a private island by next year."

Talk about common values:

DO: Discuss your beliefs, values, and relationship priorities. "In my opinion, trust and open communication are crucial in a partnership. So who are you? What values in a relationship are significant to you?

Copyright ©

AVOID: Making negative assumptions about the morals of others or being judgmental.
A nice illustration would be to say, "If you're not into monogamy, then this won't work between us."

Gratitude and interest in next plans:
DO: Express gratitude for the opportunity and show interest in the next schedule.
For example, "Thank you for a beautiful evening. Getting to know you was fun. I wish I could perform this again soon. What do you think?
AVOID: Making predictions or assuming or pressing the other person to make an instant commitment.
For instance: "I already know you're the one for me. Let's together plan for the future.
Always keep in mind that these principles are just designed to be used as a starting point. It's important to modify them to fit your personality, the conversation's flow, and the particular chemistry between you and your date. Being present, actively listening, and answering honestly are the foundations of genuine connection and good communication.

Copyright ©

Chapter 6:

Dating Techniques for Various Relationship Objectives

We'll look at several dating tactics adapted to varied relationship objectives in Chapter 6. You could have certain dating goals and ambitions if you're an older lady. This chapter will provide helpful ideas and tactics to help you navigate the dating world with confidence and purpose, regardless of whether you're looking for short-term relationships, a lifelong partner, or are open to exploring non-traditional relationship patterns. You may approach dating with clarity and make decisions that are consistent with your wants and beliefs by being aware of the particular dynamics and factors involved with each relationship goal. In this article, we'll discuss how to find a long-term partner, have fun dating, and explore non-traditional relationship types.

Copyright ©

Socializing and Casual Dating

Many older women might find their relationship aspirations fulfilled via casual dating and friendship. Here are some strategies to keep in mind:

Clarify Your Intentions:
Before beginning a casual dating relationship, take some time to spell out your goals and be open and honest with prospective partners. Make it obvious that you're looking for friendly company but aren't looking for a long-term relationship. This guarantees agreement between the parties and prevents misunderstandings.

Set limits:
To safeguard your mental well-being when casually dating, set explicit limits. Establish your comfort level in terms of the degree of emotional connection, the frequency of contact, or the need for exclusivity. You can preserve a feeling of control and prevent becoming too emotionally attached by establishing limits.

Copyright ©

Maintain open and honest conversations with your casual partners by practicing open communication. As the relationship develops, be sure to express your needs, wants, and any modifications to your expectations. This guarantees that everyone engaged is on the same page and aids in the development of mutual understanding.

Enjoy the Present:
Take advantage of the spontaneity and adaptability that casual dating offers. Don't stress about long-term obligations or aspirations for the future; just enjoy the now and your companions' company. Without placing undue strain on the relationship, be in the now and enjoy the events.

Emphasize Fun and Adventure:
Take part in activities that will make your encounters with Casual Dating Fun and Exciting. Try out new hobbies, go on adventures, and share interests with your companions. Stress the excitement and adventure of casual dating so that you may create lasting relationships.

Be Strict: Although the term "casual dating" suggests a loser attitude, it's still necessary to be picky when it comes to your dates. Select people that respect you, share your beliefs, and are interested in similar things as you are. Being picky makes sure that you only interact with people who will be fun and mutually fulfilling.

Put Self-Care First:
When casually dating, put self-care first. Maintain your physical and mental health by adopting healthy routines, making time for introspection, and taking part in soul-nourishing activities. Self-care improves your well-being as a whole and makes it easier for you to negotiate casual relationships with confidence.

Manage Expectations:
Be aware that casual dating could not result in a commitment or exclusivity over the long run. Maintain reasonable expectations for your casual relationships and refrain from imposing them on them. Recognize that casual dating is often fleeting, and be ready for the chance that relationships might terminate.

Keep It Real:

Copyright ©

When casually dating, be loyal to who you are and what you need. To preserve a casual relationship, avoid trying to be someone you're not or sacrificing your morals. Adopt a genuine stance to draw in partners that value you for who you are.

Self-awareness Exercise:

Consistently check in with yourself to determine how casual dating affects your emotional well-being. Tell yourself the truth about your emotions and desires. It's acceptable to reevaluate and make adjustments in line with your changing requirements if you discover that casual dating is no longer satisfying or suited for you.

These techniques can help you maintain a healthy emotional balance while engaging in casual dating and companionship with clarity, confidence, and fun.

Copyright ©

Finding a Long-Term Partner

The following are some approaches to take into account if you're looking for a lifelong partner:

Consider Your Relationship Goals:
Give some thought to your relationship objectives and the traits you want in a lifelong spouse. Think about your own beliefs, passions, and defining characteristics of your lifestyle. You may better connect your dating attempts with your intended results by reflecting on yourself.

Be Open to New Experiences:
When looking for a lifelong relationship, be open to new opportunities and push yourself to new limits. Attend social gatherings, sign up for organizations or groups that share your interests, or try online dating services designed especially for those looking for long-term partnerships. You may improve your chances of finding someone who shares your beliefs and objectives by being open to new experiences.

Prioritize Compatibility:
When searching for a life mate, consider your compatibility with their

values, aspirations, and way of life. Look for someone who shares your main values and objectives for the future. The basis for a solid and long-lasting relationship is compatibility.

Create a Supportive Network:
Surround yourself with friends, relatives, and others who are like-minded and who have similar dating aspirations. Participating in a community of like-minded people may provide you with emotional support, guidance, and connections to other people who may share your beliefs and interests.

Practice Being Patient:
It often takes time and patience to find a life mate. A relationship should not be entered into hastily out of need or worry about being alone. Give yourself the time you need to meet someone who genuinely fits your aspirations and trust the process.

Declare Your Intentions Clearly express your want to be in a serious long-term partnership.
Early on, be careful to express your objectives to prospective partners in clear terms to ensure that you are on the same page. By doing this, you may avoid

Copyright ©

spending time with people who might not be looking for the same degree of commitment.

Foster emotional connection with possible partners by putting in the time and effort necessary. Openly express your emotions, views, and life experiences, and exhort others to do the same. A long-term relationship requires trust and a deeper connection, both of which may be developed via emotional intimacy.

Practice Effective Communication:

In each relationship, communication is essential. Learn to be open and honest in expressing your needs, wants, and worries while also paying attention to your spouse. Effective communication helps you and your possible long-term spouse understand one another, overcome problems, and deepen your relationship.

Make Self-Care a Priority:

Throughout your dating life, make self-care a priority. Maintain your physical, mental, and spiritual well-being .Take part in enjoyable and relaxing activities, practice mindfulness, and develop self-love. You can be your best self and

Copyright ©

attract a spouse who values and respects you by taking care of yourself.

Trust Your Gut:
When evaluating prospective relationships, follow your gut. Consider your feelings toward them and if you have a real connection. Pay attention to your gut instinct and take the appropriate precautions to protect yourself if anything seems wrong or if red flags appear.

By using these tactics, you may approach the dating scene with an eye on finding a suitable long-term partner who shares your values, objectives, and aspirations for a satisfying and long-lasting relationship.

Examining Non-Traditional Relationship Models

You could be willing to consider non-traditional relationship models as an older lady. Here are some strategies to take in mind:

Copyright ©

Self-Reflection:
Give yourself some time to contemplate your preferences, requirements, and limitations in terms of unconventional romantic arrangements. Think about what fits with your beliefs and way of life and what makes you feel comfortable.

Learn About Non-Traditional Relationship Models:
Get to know non-traditional relationship models including polyamory, open partnerships, and ethical non-monogamy. Discover the foundations, dynamics, and difficulties of these models. Your ability to negotiate these connections with clarity and knowledge is aided by education.

When considering non-traditional relationship arrangements, open and honest communication is essential. Talk to prospective partners about your expectations, limits, and wants. Make sure that everyone is on the same page and ready to discuss the relationship structure regularly. The creation of clear agreements, negotiation, and mutual understanding are all made possible by effective communication.

Set limits: Identify and express your limits in the context of the unconventional relationship paradigm. Be frank about what is and is not acceptable for you and any possible partners. Rules for time management, emotional engagement, and romantic relationships are examples of boundaries. Having clear limits makes it possible to respect the requirements and comfort levels of everyone.

Develop Trust:
In every relationship, particularly non-traditional ones, trust is crucial. Encourage trust by keeping lines of communication open, being dependable, and keeping your word. To feel safe, emotionally connected, and free to explore non-traditional relationship patterns with confidence, trust is necessary.

Dealing with jealousy:
Non-traditional relationship patterns could entail many partners, which might lead to emotions of jealousy. It's important to talk about and healthily handle these feelings. When envy surfaces, practice self-awareness and be honest in your communication. Investigate methods for controlling and overcoming jealousy, such as self-evaluation,

Copyright ©

reassurance, and compersion (taking pleasure in your partner's relationships).

Self-Reflection:
As you investigate non-conventional relationship forms, be sure to reflect on yourself constantly. Analyze your emotional health, contentment, and happiness in the selected relationship arrangement. Check-in with yourself often to make sure the arrangement still meets your changing requirements and preferences.

Seek Community Support:
Look for places where you may interact with others who share your interests in non-traditional relationship models, such as communities, support groups, or online discussion forums. Participating in conversations with others who share your experiences may provide you with advice, insights, and a feeling of community. Building a strong network of allies and navigating obstacles may both be made easier by learning from others' experiences.

Accept Personal Development: Non-traditional partnerships often call for people to pursue personal development. Be willing to learn

Copyright ©

more about who you are, what you want, and how capable you are of love and connection. Accept the chance to improve your communication abilities, emotional intelligence, and knowledge of relationship dynamics.

It's important to be loyal to yourself when you investigate non-conventional relationship styles. Throughout the process, remember your beliefs, needs, and preferences. Regarding what you want and what feels right for you, be honest with both yourself and any possible partners. Keep in mind that mutual respect and sincerity are the foundations of the most rewarding partnerships.

You may negotiate the intricacies and subtleties of non-traditional relationship models with clarity, open communication, and a dedication to personal development by putting these methods into practice. This opens up the possibility of investigating other relationship patterns that fit your personality and goals as an older woman.

Copyright ©

Copyright ©

Chapter 7:

Sexuality and Intimacy

The process of finding intimacy and navigating the world of sexuality may be a singular and liberating one for older women. As we get older, our needs, wants, and viewpoints on intimacy may change, so it's important to approach this area of our life with an optimistic and open attitude.

Our chapter "The Best Dating Advice for Older Women," Chapter 7, is devoted to guiding you through this process. We realize that intimacy includes more than simply sexual gratification; it also includes emotional ties, open communication, and a clear awareness of our own needs and limitations.

We examine the many aspects of intimacy that are pertinent to older women in this chapter. We go through methods for reclaiming your wants and desires, encouraging direct and honest

Copyright ©

communication with your spouse, and developing emotional bonds. We also cover significant subjects like sexual health and safety as well as the investigation of novel relationship paradigms that may be of interest to you.

To help you accept and appreciate your sexuality and intimacy as an older woman, we want to provide you with information, insights, and helpful guidance. You may begin on a path of rediscovery and build rewarding and personal relationships in your life by adopting a positive outlook, being aware of your needs, and encouraging open communication.

Join us as we go deeper into the areas of intimacy and sexuality in Chapter 7, giving you helpful tips and techniques to improve your relationships and welcome a more fruitful and exciting chapter of your life.

Copyright ©

Regaining Intimacy

For older women, rediscovering intimacy may be a life-changing event. Here are some strategies to consider:

Consider spending some time getting to know and understanding your wants and desires for closeness. You may determine what makes you happy and fulfilled by doing this self-reflection, which makes it easier for you to express your preferences to your spouse.

Communication:
Regaining closeness requires open and honest communication. Tell your spouse about your needs, worries, and limits. Trust, emotional connection, and a greater degree of intimacy are all fostered when a secure and judgment-free environment is created for communication.

Emotional Connection:
Give emotional closeness equal weight to physical intimacy. Engage in activities that foster emotional intimacy with your spouse to strengthen your relationships, such as deep talks, shared experiences,

and displays of love. The whole quality of the intimate connection is improved by emotional closeness.

Experiment:
Incorporate an exploratory and experimental mindset in the bedroom. Be willing to experiment with novel situations, methods, or fantasies that interest you and your partner. A feeling of exploration, mutual consent, and respect may result in fascinating discoveries and deeper closeness.

Sensuality: Make an effort to achieve closeness by using all of your senses. Investigate pursuits that heighten sensory enjoyment, such as massage, sensual touch, aromatherapy, or using music and lighting to create a sensuous ambiance. Intimacy and connection may be increased through paying attention to sensory sensations.

Copyright ©

Examining Sexual Health and Safety

For older women, investigating sexual health and safety is essential. Here are some strategies to consider:

Education and Awareness:

Keep up to date on issues relating to older women's sexual health. Find information about aging-related changes, such as menopause, hormonal changes, and medical disorders. Recognize the potential effects these circumstances may have on your sexual health and, if necessary, seek the right medical guidance.

Schedule regular checkups with your healthcare practitioner to keep an eye on your sexual health.

Discuss any worries or inquiries you may have, and get advice on preserving your sexual health.

Use condoms or other barrier techniques to protect against sexually transmitted infections (STIs) while engaging in safe sex. If you're starting a new sexual relationship, think about talking to your partner about STI testing and having open discussions about sexual health.

Emotional Safety:

When entering into close relationships, give emotional safety a priority. Make sure you are with someone that respects, values and listens to you. Be sure to express your needs and limits, and pay attention to those of your spouse.

Consent and limits:

When having intimate contact, put the highest priority on obtaining consent and upholding individual limits. Ask your spouse for their clear permission and express your aspirations. communicate often to guarantee continuous comfort and consent.

Building Emotional Bonds

A vital component of intimacy is the nurturing of emotional bonds. Here are some strategies to consider:

To fully comprehend your partner's ideas, emotions, and desires, engage in active listening. Give them your whole attention, refrain from passing judgment,

Copyright ©

and reply with sympathy and understanding. This encourages a stronger emotional bond and builds mutual support.

Quality Time:

Schedule time specifically for nurturing your emotional connection. Take part in activities that you two find enjoyable and that promote bonding and meaningful discourse. To do this, you may go on walks, have meals together, enjoy hobbies together, or just set aside time for sincere chats.

gratitude:

Regularly express your partner's gratitude. Thank them for being in your life, appreciate their efforts, and compliment their good characteristics.

The development of emotional relationships can be greatly aided by expressions of gratitude.

Honesty and Vulnerability:

Talk to your spouse honestly and openly about your emotions, ideas, and vulnerabilities. Tell them about your aspirations, worries, and desires so that you may develop a closer emotional connection with them. A secure environment for emotional development and connection is created when both partners are willing to be vulnerable.

Resolution of Conflict:
Although disagreements will always arise in relationships, how you handle them emotionally may have a significant influence. When resolving arguments or misunderstandings, use effective communication, active listening, and empathy. Prioritize preserving a strong emotional connection while seeking solutions that will satisfy both parties.

Support and Encouragement:
Provide your spouse with support and encouragement at both happy and difficult moments. Be their supporter, a listening ear, and a helping hand when required. The link between you is forged and strengthened when you provide your undying support.

Remember that emotional closeness goes beyond sexual intimacy when discussing intimacy outside of the bedroom. Outside of the bedroom, take part in emotional-connection-promoting activities like long talks, similar interests, or deeds of compassion. By

Copyright ©

fostering emotional closeness throughout your relationship, you profoundly strengthen your bond.

Practice Self-Care:
Fostering emotional connections with your spouse requires taking care of your own emotional needs. Set aside time for self-care practices that will restore your energy, lower your stress level, and support emotional stability. You will be more able to improve your relationship when you are emotionally stable and satisfied.

Celebrate Relationship Achievements:
Take the time to acknowledge and honor your relationship's accomplishments. Recognize and enjoy these occasions with your loved ones, whether it's a little victory or a significant milestone. This strengthens your emotional bond by encouraging a feeling of gratitude and delight.

Continuous Growth and Learning:
Adopt an attitude that your relationship is always growing and learning. Recognize that throughout time, emotional ties may alter and develop. Keep an open mind, go out on new adventures with your partner, and make time for your relationship and

Copyright ©

personal growth. This dedication to development enables your emotional bond to flourish and adjust to the changing circumstances of your relationship.

By putting these techniques into practice, you may develop a solid and satisfying emotional bond with your partner, developing a closeness that transcends just physical desire. Fostering emotional connections improves the overall quality of your relationship and helps you both feel content and happy for a long time.

Copyright ©

Chapter 8

Understanding that beauty is determined by confidence and self-care rather than age

Older women must embrace the notion that beauty is ageless when it comes to dating. Contrary to popular belief, beauty is not determined by one's age but rather by one's self-confidence, self-care, and acceptance of their individuality. With an emphasis on the idea that beauty is a timeless quality that can be strengthened through self-assurance and nurture, this chapter offers a resource for dating guidance.

It's crucial to develop a mentality that values your natural attractiveness and understands the need for self-assurance as an older lady. You'll accomplish this because you'll emit magnetic energy that attracts people of all ages to you. To assist you embrace

Copyright ©

your beauty and move through the dating world with elegance and poise, we will go into further detail about this idea in the paragraphs that follow.

Embracing Self-Acceptance:
Self-acceptance is the first step toward real beauty. Be proud of your maturity, knowledge, and other personal traits that make you who you are.

Setting Self-Care as a Priority:
Maintaining your physical and mental health is essential for exuding beauty. Take part in activities that are good for your body, mind, and spirit, such as meditation, exercise, and following your favorite hobbies.

Confident Dressing:
Wear things that make you feel at ease and assured. Dressing in a manner that expresses your personality and builds your confidence is important.

Stressing Inner Beauty:
Real beauty transcends outward appearance. Nurture your kindness, compassion, and sincerity to enhance your inner beauty. These characteristics will come

Copyright ©

through and increase your allure in the eyes of others.

Recognize and appreciate all of your successes, no matter how large or little. Your life's experiences and accomplishments, which highlight your tenacity, tenacity, and personal development, add to your special attractiveness.

Positive Influence Surroundings:

Surround yourself with uplifting, motivating individuals. Select friends and lovers who will help you on your road to confidence by appreciating and valuing you.

Engage in activities that advance your general well-being to maintain a healthy lifestyle. Eat a balanced diet, remain hydrated, get enough sleep, and make regular exercise a priority. These routines will increase your luminosity and vigor.

Experiment with haircuts, cosmetics, and accessories that showcase your features and personality to improve your sense of style. Developing a look that makes you feel confident and attractive might help you look better.

Copyright ©

Gratitude for Aging:

Aging is a normal aspect of life. Accept the changes that occur with being older and see them as proof of the knowledge and experiences you have attained. The ability to age gracefully will allow you to radiate beauty from the inside out.

Using Positive Self-Talk:

Refute negative self-talk and swap it out with positive statements. Remind yourself of your value, charm, and special attributes. Develop a mentality of appreciation for and self-love.

Radiating Confidence:

Self-assurance has a powerful pull. Reflect on your actions, develop as a person, and be open to new experiences as you work to increase your self-confidence. In your conversations and connections, let your confidence come through.

Sensitivity has no age restrictions, so embrace it. Explore your emotions and wants while embracing your sexuality. Make a connection to your sexuality and express it in ways that are natural to you.

Stressing Inner Strength:

Be aware of and grateful for the inner strength you have grown to possess through time. When confronted with difficulties, rely on your tenacity and resolve, knowing that your beauty is enhanced by your strength.

Developing a Positive Attitude:

Develop a positive attitude that appreciates the beauty in each stage of life. Concentrate on the present and the possibilities it offers. Accept the voyage of self-discovery and personal development, understanding that every encounter adds to your total grace and knowledge.

Embracing Authenticity:

Be honest with yourself and accept who you are. Avoid attempting to live up to social expectations or too unattainable beauty standards. Accept your individuality and let your actual self emerge.

Keep in mind that beauty is not limited by age but rather reflects your self-assurance, self-care, and acceptance of your uniqueness. You may attract people's attention by establishing self-acceptance, putting self-care first, and celebrating your accomplishments. Gracefully accept your aging

Copyright ©

process and enjoy the beauty that comes with each new year.

In conclusion, age is not a factor in attractiveness. It's a trait that's characterized by assurance, self-care, and acceptance of one's characteristics. You may start a great dating adventure as an older woman by focusing on self-acceptance, enhancing your inner and exterior attractiveness, and radiating honesty. Accept your natural beauty and let it radiate for everyone to see.

Personal well-being and self-care

Making self-care a priority:

It's important to look after yourself if you want to date and form lasting relationships. Making your health a high priority and maintaining a healthy balance between your physical, emotional, and mental needs are examples of prioritizing self-care.

Setting limits, cultivating self-compassion, and partaking in enjoyable pursuits are all part of this. Making self-care a priority not only improves your well-being but also attracts others because of the pleasant vibes you exude.

Preserving Good Mental and Physical Health:

Your total well-being is highly influenced by your physical and mental health, which may also have a big effect on your dating life. To maintain your physical health, it's important to practice frequent physical exercise, consume a healthy diet, and obtain adequate sleep. Additionally, maintaining your mental health by engaging in mindfulness practices, getting help when necessary, and managing stress may help you think positively and engage with prospective partners more effectively.

Adopting a Positive Mentality:

When it comes to dating as an older woman, having a positive outlook is a great weapon. Developing optimism, thankfulness, and perseverance in the face of difficulties is a part of embracing positivity. It entails putting an end to self-deprecating thoughts, embracing self-love, and going into relationships

Copyright ©

with an open heart and mind. A positive outlook attracts good encounters and enables you to embark on the dating adventure with zeal and confidence.

Self-reflection exercises:

To maintain self-care and personal well-being, it is crucial to set aside time for introspection. Consider your relationship ideals, aspirations, and objectives. Consider your true needs and desires in a companion. You'll be guided by this self-awareness to make decisions that are consistent with your real self, which will result in more satisfying interactions.

Establish Limits:

To create your boundaries and safeguard your emotional well-being, you must practice self-care. Potential partners should be made aware of your limits and your wants and expectations. Healthy boundaries help you build a relationship based on mutual respect and guarantee that your needs are satisfied while dating.

Take Part in Activities You Love:

Make time for your cheerful and contentment-inducing activities. Hobbies and interests provide

Copyright ©

you the chance to meet others who share your interests as well as to feed your spirit. Pursuing your hobbies enables you to bring your genuine self to the dating world, whether it is through joining a book club, taking a culinary class, or volunteering for a cause you're passionate about.

Self-compassion exercises:

As you go through the dating process, be gentle to yourself. Recognize that not every date will be the ideal fit, and that's alright. Recognize that dating is a process with ups and downs and treat yourself with kindness and forgiveness. Celebrate your accomplishments and skills, and try not to be too harsh on yourself when things don't go according to plan.

Maintain Supportive Relationships Around You:

Develop your connections with friends, family, and a welcoming community. As you navigate the dating scene, having a strong support system and good influences around you may provide you with emotional support, motivation, and useful guidance. With the knowledge that you are not traveling alone, rely on these connections for support, and feel free to share your experiences.

Practice stress management and mindfulness:

Utilize mindfulness techniques in your routine to lower stress and maintain present-moment awareness. You may remain centered and focused by practicing mindfulness, whether it be via meditation, deep breathing exercises, or relaxing hobbies. Maintaining personal well-being and approaching dating with a clear and composed head need effective stress management.

Accept growth and take lessons from it:

Consider every dating encounter as a chance for development and self-discovery. Draw lessons from both successful and unsuccessful experiences to help you hone your preferences, better understand your beliefs, and determine what you want in a companion. Adopt the perspective that every conversation, whether fruitful or fruitless, offers insightful information that advances your development and path toward making meaningful connections.

Develop Your Gratitude:

Develop a spirit of thankfulness as you go through the dating process. Keep your attention on the good outcomes of each event, and be grateful for the chances that come your way. Thank yourself for the experiences gained, the relationships created, and the personal development brought about by venturing outside of your comfort zone. You may change your viewpoint and attract more happiness into your dating life by cultivating an attitude of appreciation.

Keep Yourself Pure:

Above all, be loyal to who you are and remain real throughout the dating process. It might be tempting to change who you are to match someone else's standards or to sacrifice your principles to win over a possible mate. Genuine relationships, however, are based on respect and acceptance between parties. Accept your individuality, uphold your morals, and have faith in who you are as a person. By being yourself, you draw partners that value and respect you for who you are.

To have a successful and enjoyable dating experience as an older woman, keep in mind that self-care and general well-being are crucial

Copyright ©

foundations. Your dating experience will be improved by prioritizing your physical, mental, and emotional well-being, maintaining a positive outlook, and embracing personal development. These actions will also improve your general happiness and well-being. With self-assurance, self-love, and a conviction that you may discover a rewarding relationship, embrace this new chapter in your life.

Copyright ©

chapter 9

Dating while parenting

Having kids and dating as an older woman comes with certain obligations. This chapter will examine how dating affects your kids and provide advice on how to talk to them about your dating life. You may strike a healthy balance between your personal life and your position as a parent by handling this area of your dating adventure with care and respect.

Taking Your Children's Well-Being Into Account When Dating

It's important to take your kids' needs into account before starting a dating adventure. Understand that adding a new partner to their life may be exciting and difficult. Spend some time evaluating how it could affect their feelings, daily routines, and family relationships.

Consider the ages and developmental stages of your children. Older children could have their worries and ideas, while younger children might want more confidence and time to get used to the notion of you

Copyright ©

dating. Be ready for a variety of responses and feelings from your kids, and treat the circumstance with compassion and understanding.

Balance your parenting obligations while making sure you are emotionally prepared to date. Your dating life shouldn't ever make your kids feel ignored or subordinate. Create a support network to assist you in successfully juggling your personal and family responsibilities.

Discussing Dating with Your Children

When talking to your kids about your dating life, be open and honest with them. Consider the following important factors:

Timing:

Pick a suitable time for the talk. Find a time when you and your kids can talk unhurriedly and comfortably.

Age-Appropriate Communication:

Copyright ©

Tailor your communication to your children's age and level of comprehension. To make sure kids can understand and assimilate the information, use language and ideas that are suitable for their age.

Reassurance:

Reassure your children that your love and dedication to them are steadfast and that dating does not change that. Reiterate how important your connection with them is.

Give your kids a chance to share their opinions on your dating life by actively listening to them. Pay close attention, acknowledge their feelings, and take any worries they may have into account.

limits:

Talk about your dating life's limits and expectations. Assure your kids that their limits will always be respected and that any future partners must do the same.

Copyright ©

Introducing Your Children to a New Partner

Parenting responsibilities and dating obligations must be balanced.

It might be difficult to introduce a new partner and maintain parental obligations while dating an older woman with kids. In this chapter, we'll discuss how to introduce a new partner to your kids and provide advice on how to manage both your dating life and your parental duties. You may create a happy atmosphere for both your love relationships and your children by negotiating these factors with caution and open communication.

Telling Your Kids About a New Partner

Copyright ©

A crucial milestone in your dating process is introducing a new spouse to your kids. Here are some helpful tips for completing this process:
Select the right moment to introduce your new spouse to your kids. Give the relationship enough time to grow, and make sure you and your partner are equally comfortable taking this next step.

Informal Introduction:
To reduce stress, start with a calm, informal environment. Think about engaging your spouse in activities that your kids like. This strategy promotes natural interactions and enables everyone to get to know one another in a relaxed setting.

Honest and open communication with your kids about your new spouse should be a top priority.
Encourage children to express their views and emotions and to ask questions. Reassure them that their ideas count and allay any fears they may have.
Patience and Understanding: Recognize that it can take some time for your kids to get used to the new dynamics in the household. As they work through their feelings and embrace your dating life, be patient and encouraging.

Copyright ©

Using your dating experiences as a chance to educate your kids about healthy relationships, communication, and respect is known as "role modeling healthy relationships." Show them what it means to put your pleasure first while yet keeping a healthy balance with your family.

Seeking Professional Support:
You could think about getting advice from a family therapist or counselor if you discover that your kids are having trouble understanding the idea of your dating life or if there are serious difficulties. They may provide insightful viewpoints and practical solutions for dealing with your family's particular demands.

Keep in mind that every family is different, so there isn't a single best way to talk to your kids about your dating life. Adapt these suggestions to your situation, and always place a high value on courteous, open communication to create a nurturing atmosphere for your kids.

Honoring Feelings and Emotions:
Throughout the dating process, validate and recognize your children's emotions. Encourage

children to communicate all of their feelings, whether they are happy or sad, and reassure them that they are essential and genuine. Make an environment where people feel comfortable talking about their worries or fears.

Transparency and Honesty:
Be open and honest about your dating experiences with your kids. Don't overshare or subject the individuals you're dating to needless information; just provide relevant facts. Honesty promotes a feeling of security within the family and helps to create trust.

Maintaining Consistency and Stability:
While dating brings about some changes to the family dynamic, make an effort to keep your children's life consistent and stable. Keep to your regular schedule, spend quality time with your kids, and reassure them that they are still a top priority in your life.

Find a balance between your dating life and your responsibilities as a parent. Make sure to set out time just for your kids to strengthen the link between you two. Show that you can effectively manage your

Copyright ©

personal life while still taking care of your parental duties.

Reverse the roles and let your kids influence your dating choices. Respect their viewpoints and ideas since they could provide important information or observations that you might have missed. When deciding on possible partners or the time of introductions, take their advice into account.

Gradual Introductions:

When it's time to introduce your kids to a new spouse, go at their pace and consider how comfortable they are. To reduce any possible pressure, schedule easygoing meetings in comfortable, neutral locations. Allow your spouse and your kids' connection to grow gradually over time.

Patience and Flexibility:

Recognize that it can take your kids some time to become used to your dating life. Be understanding of their feelings and behaviors, and be adaptable while attending to their needs. As required, modify your strategy in light of the particular dynamics in your household.

Copyright ©

Reassurance of Love and Support:
Throughout the dating process, continuously reaffirm your kid's love and support. Remind them that your desire to date doesn't change how much you adore them. Assure them that you are always there for them and that you care about them.

Setting a Good Example:
Be a good example for your kids by acting responsibly when you go out on dates. Show respect, good boundaries, and healthy communication in your interactions. By doing this, you impart to them important knowledge about what to anticipate in their upcoming relationships.

Regular Check-Ins:
As you continue your dating life, keep the lines of communication open with your kids. Check-in with them often to gauge how they are feeling and handle any potential worries. This constant communication helps to build trust and makes sure that their requirements are understood and satisfied.

Remind everyone of the value of respecting one another's boundaries. Your kids may need time and

Copyright ©

space to get used to the new dynamic. Encourage your spouse to be patient and empathetic while letting your kids lead the way in developing their bond.

Continue to emphasize spending quality time with your kids, making sure they know how much you cherish and adore them. Make time for one-on-one interaction with each kid regularly to sustain healthy parent-child ties.

Reinforce Family Values:

Talk with your spouse about the significance of preserving and promoting family values. Work together to establish a setting that promotes your parenting philosophy and the development and well-being of your kids.

As the connection develops, engage your kids in choices that might have an impact on them, including combining families or making substantial life changes. To make sure that their opinions are heard and valued, ask for their feedback and pay attention to their worries.

Seek Support:

If you run into problems or have worries when introducing someone, think about getting advice from a family therapist or counselor. They may provide knowledgeable perspectives and approaches to help everyone involved adjust smoothly.

Checking In Frequently:
Keep the lines of communication open with your spouse and children. Check-in with both parties often to gauge how they are feeling and resolve any potential problems. Mutual respect, trust, and understanding are fostered by this constant conversation.

Gradual Inclusion:
Permit your spouse to progressively become involved in your kids' life. Encourage joint endeavors, family trips, and special events that foster kinship and provide shared memories.

Honoring Children's Emotions:
Throughout the process, validate and recognize your children's emotions. Encourage them to voice any doubts or worries they may have. As people negotiate their emotions during this time of change, be sympathetic and empathetic.

Be a Team:

Work together with your spouse to develop a consistent parenting strategy. Make sure that you and your partner have the same standards for the welfare of your kids. To promote continuity and stability, put up a unified front.

Flexibility in Scheduling:
It takes flexibility to balance dating and parenting duties. When it comes to scheduling, be understanding and flexible, making sure to set out time for both your spouse and children. Find a balance that enables you to take care of your children while fostering your relationship.

Maintain open and honest conversations with your spouse about the rewards and difficulties of juggling your dating life and parental obligations. Discussing limits, expectations, and the value of flexibility can help to create a strong and dependable connection.

Shared Parenting Responsibilities:
When suitable and agreed upon by all parties, consider how you might engage your spouse in parenting duties. This may foster a feeling of cohesion and a common dedication to your kids' welfare.

Copyright ©

Prioritize your well-being and get help when you need it. Being a good parent and spouse requires taking care of your physical and emotional needs. Lean on dependable friends, family, or support networks for advice, inspiration, and help when needed.

Recognize that quality time with your children is more important than the amount of time spent with them. By participating in meaningful activities, encouraging open communication, and making enduring memories, you can make the most of the time you have together.

Flexibility and Adaptability:

Be aware that sometimes unanticipated events happen that necessitate changing your dating and parenting plans. Stay versatile and flexible, coming up with original ideas that take into account the requirements and objectives of everyone.

Healthy Relationship Role Modeling:

Show your kids what it means to juggle parental duties with a happy loving relationship. Show kids the value of open communication, mutual respect, and putting family members' well-being first.

Copyright ©

Trusting Your Gut Feelings:
As a parent and as a person, trust your gut feelings. You are the most qualified to make choices for your children's needs and welfare since you know them the best. Know that you can manage the challenges of parenting while pursuing your pleasure.

Celebrate Milestones Together:
As a blended family, be proud of your partner's and your children's accomplishments. Together, celebrate milestones, victories, and holidays to foster a feeling of community and belonging.

Evaluate your parenting duties and dating obligations with one another regularly. Be ready to change and adapt as necessary to guarantee the happiness and health of your children as well as your love relationships.

Ultimately, keep in mind to accept the love and pleasure that may result from balancing your need for companionship with your parental responsibilities. You may cultivate a supportive atmosphere where love and happiness can develop by being honest with one another, understanding one another, and being adaptable.

As an older woman, juggling dating obligations and parental duties calls for thoughtful deliberation and

Copyright ©

good communication. You may achieve a pleasing and satisfying balance for yourself, your kids, and your spouse by adopting these tactics into your trip.

Here are a few realistic instances that show how an older woman may juggle dating and parenting responsibilities:

Say something along the lines of, "Hey, just wanted to let you know that I'll be going out on a date night with [partner's name] on Friday. I have a babysitter lined up since I cherish our time together. Feel welcome to contact me if you want any assistance or have any queries.

As an example of incorporating your kids, invite your spouse to take part in a family activity, like a movie night or a day at the park. This enables interaction between your children and your spouse in a comfortable setting. Say something like, "Hey, I was considering going to the park on Saturday. It would be wonderful if you could come along.

Together, we may have fun and learn more about one another.

Flexible Scheduling Example: If you have limited or shared custody of your children, think of creative ways to balance your and your spouse's time with them. If your children are in school, you may plan a lunch or coffee date for your lunch break. In this way, you may fulfill your parenting duties and still have quality time with your spouse.

If you're considering taking your relationship to the next level, for example, include your kids in the decision-making process. Get their opinions and suggestions by asking about family mingling or major life changes. By incorporating them, you show that their opinions are valued. Say something like, "I've been considering [partner's name] moving in with us. What do you make of that? As an example, I want to ensure that everyone is at ease and content with the choice.

Setting aside devoted one-on-one time with each of your children can help to build the link between parents and children. It might be as simple as

Copyright ©

sharing a pastime, watching a movie, or going for a stroll. Make it clear to them that you value their unique demands and interests.

Keep in mind that although these examples are designed to serve as a guide, it's crucial to modify them to fit your situation and your children's requirements. Finding the ideal balance takes adaptability, clear communication, and a readiness to change as circumstances dictate since every family dynamic is unique.

Copyright ©

Copyright ©

Chapter 10

Building Step-Relationships and Blending Families

The idea of mixing families and creating step-relationships is common when an older woman enters a new relationship. This chapter examines the special difficulties and interactions that may occur when integrating houses, kids, and various family configurations. Patience, compassion, and open communication are necessary for navigating these complications. It is possible to construct peaceful blended families and forge solid step-relationships by confronting the difficulties head-on and encouraging a supportive atmosphere.

Navigating Blended Family Challenges:

Recognize Diverse Points of View:
Blended families often include members with various racial origins, parenting philosophies, and expectations. Recognize and accept these variations,

Copyright ©

enabling each member of the family to voice their opinions and participate in decision-making.

Open Up Communication Channels:
For blended families to navigate their obstacles, clear and open communication is essential. To create a climate of trust and understanding, encourage family members to express their ideas, worries, and emotions. Regular family gatherings or one-on-one chats may provide a forum for candid discussion.

Develop Connections Gradually:
Family blending takes time and patience. Relationships should be allowed to grow gradually; do not hurry it. Encourage family members to participate in activities that foster bonding and shared experiences, as well as quality time spent together.

Create fresh family customs:
Families that have been blended might establish new customs that pay homage to both the past and the present. A feeling of togetherness and belonging may be fostered by creating special rituals or events that engage the whole family.

Respect for privacy and boundaries:

Managing personal boundaries and privacy issues is a challenge when families merge. Encourage candid conversations regarding each person's desire for privacy and personal space. The blended family unit feels safe and secure when these boundaries are respected.

Seek Expert Assistance:
The difficulties of integrating families might sometimes need expert advice. Family therapists or counselors may provide helpful viewpoints, resources, and tactics to address particular problems and promote constructive family communication.

Make inclusion and acceptance a priority:
Make sure that everyone in the blended family feels welcomed and included. Celebrate each person's originality and uniqueness to create a welcoming workplace.

Unified parenting and co-parenting:
Co-parenting and creating consistent parenting philosophies are crucial when there are children involved. A stable and encouraging atmosphere for

the kids is facilitated by consistency, cooperation, and respect between the parents and stepparents.

Keep your relationships with your stepchildren healthy.

It takes time to establish healthy bonds between stepparents and stepchildren. Find ways to connect via shared hobbies or activities, encourage open communication, and respect each other's limits. Allow these connections to grow organically over time.

Fostering solid parent-child relationships

In a mixed family, encourage the relationship between the children's biological parents and them. To preserve a close bond and make sure the kids feel loved and supported, parents should promote quality one-on-one time with their kids.

Seek Empathy and Understanding:

Blended families often experience particular difficulties, therefore it's critical to tackle these difficulties with respect and understanding. Each family member may go through the process of adjusting and processing their emotions. Be kind

Copyright ©

and patient with everyone as they adjust to the changes and the new family dynamics.

Promote adaptability and flexibility:

When families are blended, flexibility and adaptation are necessary due to unforeseen circumstances or changes. Encourage an adaptable mentality and embrace the need for flexibility in schedules, habits, and expectations to meet the changing requirements of mixed families.

Honor your accomplishments and milestones:

Celebrate each family member's accomplishments, anniversaries, and victories. By praising and acknowledging each person's achievements, you create an environment that is constructive and encouraging.

Copyright ©

Creating Positive Bonds with Adult Children

It is crucial to understand the complexities of creating wholesome connections with adult children from past partnerships while beginning new relationships as an older lady. This chapter examines the difficulties that might result from mixing families and provides suggestions for building good relationships with adult children. You may have solid and dependable relationships with your adult children while pursuing your love interests if you comprehend their viewpoints, engage in open communication and respect limits.

Recognize and Validate Their Emotions:
It's crucial to respect and support your adult children's sentiments while bringing a new spouse into your life. Recognize that a variety of feelings, such as trepidation, protectiveness, or even animosity, may be experienced by them. Allow them the room to voice their worries, and then listen to them with compassion and understanding.

Maintain Honest and Open Communication:

Throughout the dating process, keep the channels of communication open with your adult children. Be open and honest about your goals, and talk to your family about how your new relationship could change things. Encourage your kids to express their ideas and worries, and listen to them with respect and tolerance.

Respect for Personal Choices and Boundaries:

Respect your adult children's limits and decisions. Recognize that their standards for relationships, lives, and ideals may vary. Respect their autonomy in making the judgments that are best for them and refrain from forcing your own opinions on them.

Gradually introduce your partner:

Introduce your new spouse to your adult children gradually as it seems right. Start with informal and relaxed encounters, like a shared hobby or a group excursion. This makes it possible for everyone to organically get to know one another and form bonds over time.

Copyright ©

Encourage individual connections:

Encourage your spouse and your adult children to have their relationships. Encourage them to interact, take part in activities they have in common, and get to know one another better. Let connections grow naturally rather than pressing or forcing them.

Address disagreements and issues:

If issues or worries occur between your new partner and your grown children, deal with them as soon as possible in a positive way. Encourage open dialogues where all parties may air their opinions and try to come up with solutions that are acceptable to everybody. Find a middle ground and promote mutual understanding.

Maintain Priorities and Balance:

Maintain a healthy balance between your adult children's needs and your new love engagement. Make sure you keep putting energy, time, and emotional support into both aspects of your life. Set priorities for your obligations and work out how to take care of your partner's and your kids' demands at the same time.

Copyright ©

Clarify Your Expectations:

Establish explicit guidelines for limits, mutual participation in one other's life, and attendance at family activities with your spouse and your adult children. To prevent misunderstandings and unreasonable expectations, be transparent about everyone's duties and responsibilities.

If necessary, seek professional assistance:

Consider getting professional help, such as family therapy or counseling, if disagreements continue or your relationships with your adult children become strained. A qualified expert may provide direction and tactics for negotiating challenging family dynamics and enhancing communication.

Observe Family Traditions and Milestones:

Even when you seek your love relationship, keep up with family customs and milestones with your adult children. Make an effort to include your spouse in these occasions so that the family may feel inclusive and united.

Copyright ©

Self-care and emotional well-being exercises:

When dealing with adult children, it is vital to look after your own emotional needs. Take part in self-care activities that promote your mental and emotional well-being, such as writing, exercise, or meditation. When you put self-care first, you can be a balanced and upbeat influence in all of your relationships.

Real-world examples

Hypothetical situation: Your adult kid questions the motives of your new spouse.

In response, pay close attention to your child's worries and acknowledge their sentiments. Have a direct discussion with them about their concerns. Talk about your thoughts and experiences with your partner's personality and motivations. To promote greater understanding and allay their fears, offer to set up a meeting between your kid and your partner.

Example: Your adult kid is uncomfortable discussing family gatherings with your new partner.

Respond by letting your youngster know that you understand their discomfort and that their emotions

Copyright ©

are real. Give your kid alternatives like gradually including your partner in family activities or organizing separate gatherings where they will feel more comfortable. Respect their limits and underline the need of preserving close family ties.

Hypothetical situation: Your adult kid complains that your new spouse is too involved in decisions.
Organize a family gathering to define duties and expectations for each family member. Encourage open conversation and give your kid a chance to express their thoughts and worries. To show that choices are taken collectively while respecting individual limits, try to reach compromises that take into account everyone's points of view.

Situation: You believe your new partner's presence overshadows your adult kid.
To strengthen your relationship and reassure your adult kid of their significance in your life, prioritize spending quality time with them one-on-one. Encourage interactions that improve your friendship with them. Help them realize that your love and connection to them are unaffected by the presence of your new partner.

Copyright ©

Situation: Your adult kid and your new partner get into a fight.

Response: Adopt a neutral stance and promote frank communication between the two sides. Encourage a polite dialogue so both parties may voice their opinions and concerns. Make sure everyone feels heard and understood by mediating the dialogue. Encourage them to cooperate and strive to create a harmonious connection.

Hypothetical situation: Your adult kid is reluctant to welcome your new partner into the family.

Answer: Discuss the value of inclusion and acceptance with your adult kid in an open and honest dialogue. Share your new partner's good traits and experiences with them to allay their fears. To promote a stronger connection and understanding, encourage them to spend quality time together.

Hypothetical situation: Your adult child disapproves of how your new spouse treats them or their kids.

Encourage your adult kid and your partner to communicate openly. Encourage a polite dialogue in which both participants can voice their opinions.

Copyright ©

Focus on similar objectives and respect for one another to assist in bringing them together. Suggest family therapy sessions if required to address any underlying problems.

The possibility of changes to their inheritance or family dynamics brought on by your new spouse has your adult kid feeling intimidated.

Response: Assure your adult kid that you still love and support them despite the presence of your new spouse. Transparency is ensured by being upfront and honest about any worries you may have about an inheritance or money difficulties. To guide you through these delicate conversations and arrive at solutions you can both agree on, think about consulting an estate planner or lawyer.

Example: When you spend time with your new companion, your adult kid feels excluded or left out.

Reaction: Discuss the value of balance and time management with your adult kid. Assure them that they will always have a special place in your life. To improve your connection with your kid and allay any emotions of neglect, schedule specific one-on-one time. To assist promote a feeling of inclusion, involve them in events or trips that also include your new spouse.

Copyright ©

Situation: As you want to start a new relationship, your adult kid raises worries about their engagement in your life and position.

In response, acknowledge your child's worries and stress that you still love and support them. Reiterate that maintaining a new romance does not weaken your connection to them. Find methods to include their opinions and engagement in your life and decision-making processes, and talk about how their role could change.

It's important to keep in mind that developing strong connections with adult children takes constant communication, empathy, and a willingness to listen to their issues. You may negotiate the difficulties and build happy connections within your blended family by keeping the lines of communication open, understanding their emotions, and looking for common ground.

An adult kid of yours has expressed worries about their interactions with their step-siblings or about possible disputes in the blended family.

Validate your child's anxieties and underline that it's normal to be anxious about transitioning to a new family dynamic in your response. Encourage open

Copyright ©

communication and provide family members with the opportunity to connect and get to know one another. As they negotiate these interactions, provide them with support and advice and reaffirm the fact that forming bonds takes time and effort

Common Strategies for overcoming it

Respect for Current Relationships:

The ties stepchildren and grandkids already have with their birth parents or grandparents should be respected. Recognizing the significance and relevance of these relationships, encourage and promote them. Keep your expectations and comparisons reasonable so as not to put undue pressure on these connections.

Make fusion-style family traditions:

Create new customs that combine those of your extended family, your new spouse, and your stepchildren. Include your stepchildren and grandkids in the development of these customs and invite them to provide their thoughts and comments.

Copyright ©

The feeling of cohesion and belonging among the blended family is fostered by these shared experiences.

Be an Example:
Be an inspiration to your stepchildren and grandkids by setting a good example. Show compassion, kindness, and effective communication. Respect people and engage in constructive dispute resolution. Your behaviors and attitudes will have a long-lasting impact on them and aid in the development of their social abilities.

If necessary, seek professional assistance:
Do not be afraid to seek professional assistance if you have difficulties or disputes while trying to establish relationships with your stepchildren and grandkids. Family therapists or counselors may provide helpful direction and coping mechanisms for navigating challenging family relationships. They may assist you in addressing particular problems, enhancing communication, and fostering stronger ties within the blended family.

Copyright ©

Be adaptable and flexible:

Recognize that throughout time, family relationships may alter and develop. Be willing to modify your tactics and approach as necessary. Building and sustaining strong relationships with stepchildren and grandkids requires flexibility and adaptation. Accept the chances for development and be prepared to modify as needed to suit their changing demands.

Establish Limits and Respect Privacy:

While building relationships is vital, it's also important to respect the privacy of stepchildren and grandkids and keep appropriate boundaries. Recognize that they could have dynamics and interactions that go beyond those of a mixed family. Allow them to set their limits and respect their desire for privacy.

Celebrate Special Occasions and Milestones:

Make an effort to spend holidays, milestones, and special events as a mixed family. Recognize and celebrate milestones in the lives of stepchildren and grandkids, such as birthdays, successes, or graduations. You show them your love, support, and

Copyright ©

dedication to their well-being by sharing these moments.

Keep in mind that developing meaningful connections with your stepchildren and grandkids needs time, effort, and patience. You may establish a caring and encouraging atmosphere where everyone feels valued and involved in the blended family by encouraging open communication, demonstrating real interest, respecting limits, and obtaining professional assistance when necessary.

Copyright ©

Chapter 11

Dating After a Divorce or Loss

For older women, dating after a divorce or losing a spouse may be a transformational and sometimes difficult experience. We will discuss helpful tips and guidance on navigating the dating scene after a divorce or loss in this chapter. We will go through how to move beyond former relationships, how to become emotionally ready for new relationships, how to deal with mixed families, and how to deal with step-parenting. You may enter a new chapter of love and friendship with courage and resiliency by accepting this one.

Moving on and Overcoming Old Relationships

To lay a strong basis for future connections, it is essential to go beyond prior ties. Think about the following tactics:

Copyright ©

Allow Yourself to Grieve:

Recognize your grief over the end of a prior relationship or the death of a partner, and permit yourself to do so. Permit yourself to feel the associated feelings of grief, rage, or perplexity. To help you through this process, ask close friends, family, or a therapist for assistance.

Self-Reflection:

Give yourself some time to consider the lessons you've taken away from previous relationships. Determine any trends or actions that may have had a part in the breakdown of those relationships. As you go ahead, use this self-awareness to develop and make healthy adjustments.

Accept Self-Care:

Make self-care a priority as a component of your recovery process. Engage in pleasurable pursuits like fitness, hobbies, or quality time with those we love. Your recovery process will be aided by providing for your physical, emotional, and spiritual needs.

Copyright ©

Establishing healthy limits will help you in your future relationships. With prospective partners, be clear about your requirements, wants, and deal-breakers. You can safeguard your well-being and make sure that your future relationships are consistent with your beliefs and objectives by establishing boundaries.

If necessary, get professional assistance. If you are having trouble moving over prior relationships on your own, think about getting advice from a therapist or counselor. They may provide you with resources and encouragement to help you get beyond your trauma and cultivate a more positive outlook on making new relationships.

Practice forgiveness by forgiving both yourself and others with whom you have had prior connections. It might be difficult to move on and make room for new opportunities if you hold onto anger or blame. You may let go of unfavorable feelings and make room for love and happiness by forgiving others.

Accept Personal Growth and Reinvention:

See this time in your life as a chance for personal development and reinvention. Explore new hobbies,

Copyright ©

rediscover your passions, and welcome the voyage of self-discovery. You'll be able to attract relationships that are healthier and more rewarding because of this reinvention.

Surround Yourself with Positive Support: Seek out the company of upbeat, encouraging people who will support your personal development and dating efforts. Positive impacts can help you feel more confident and will act as a support system for you while you travel.

A new relationship should not be entered into before you are emotionally prepared. Instead, do things at your own pace. Give yourself the time and space you need to recover completely and reclaim your identity. When you're ready to start dating again, go at your speed and respect your schedule.

While it's crucial to draw lessons from the past, make an effort to keep your attention on the here and now as well as the future. Accept the chances that come your way and enter into each new relationship with an open mind and heart.

Making Oneself Emotionally Prepared for New Connections

Copyright ©

Establishing emotional preparedness is essential before starting new relationships. Think about the following actions:

Clarify your dating aims by reflecting on them.
Are you looking for companionship, a dedicated long-term relationship, or are you just interested in making new friends? Knowing what you want can help you make better dating choices.

Examine your emotional condition and preparation for a new relationship honestly

Determine if you have dealt with your prior experiences and are prepared to share your heart with a new person. A good relationship may be hampered by emotional baggage or unsolved difficulties, so be mindful of these.

When deciding if you are emotionally prepared to date again, listen to your gut and trust your judgment. If you're still on the fence or uneasy, it can be a sign that you need more time to recover and put your needs first before looking for new connections.

Copyright ©

Accept Vulnerability:
Accept that being open to love again requires being vulnerable. Be prepared to lower your guard and let someone else see and get to know you. Accepting vulnerability may result in more meaningful friendships and connections.

Create a Network of Supportive Friends and Family:
Surround yourself with a network of supportive friends and family who can provide advice, inspiration, and a listening ear. Talk to them about your dating experiences and feelings, and consider their opinions when making crucial choices.

Declare Your Emotional Limits:
Be forward with prospective partners about your emotional limits. Inform them of your preferences, your wants, and any particular requirements or worries you may have. Healthy relationships may be cultivated and misunderstandings can be avoided through upfront honesty and open communication.

Make Self-Care a Priority:
As you negotiate the dating scene, make self-care a priority. Take part in activities that will refuel your

spirit and emotional state of being. This might be participating in mindfulness exercises, hobbies, outdoor activities, therapy, or counseling to promote your emotional development.

Accept Patience:
Recognize that establishing a new bond requires time and patience. Avoid jumping into relationships too quickly and let them develop on their own. As you establish a foundation of emotional connection and trust, allow yourself to go deliberately and trust the process.

Reflect on the lessons you've gained from previous relationships and use them to inform your present dating life.
Make deliberate decisions that are in line with your emotional well-being by identifying any red flags or patterns that you wish to avoid.

Celebrate your progress:
Throughout your recovery process, recognize and honor your progress. Recognize the fortitude and resiliency you have acquired via conquering obstacles in the past. Accept the knowledge you

Copyright ©

have gained and take it with you as you make new relationships.

Understanding the Dynamics of Step-Parenting and Blended Families

It takes patience, understanding, and open communication to navigate the difficulties of blended families and step-parenting if you are starting a relationship with someone who has kids or is combining families. Think about the following tactics:

Establish Trust and Respect:

It's important to establish trust and respect with your partner's kids. Spend some time getting to know each person and care about their life. Allow the connections to grow organically without pushing or hurrying the process; instead, be patient.

Transparent Communication:

Be honest and transparent with your spouse about your involvement in the lives of the kids and lay out

Copyright ©

your expectations. To show a unified face as a pair, talk about parenting philosophies, disciplining methods, and significant choices.

Respect Parental Boundaries:
Do not cross the line established by your biological parent(s) or act in a way that challenges their authority. Recognize that your role in their parenting is to support and enhance it, not to replace or outdo it.

Working together to make decisions and share parenting duties is an important element of step-parenting. Cooperate to construct a consistent strategy and produce a peaceful atmosphere for the kids. Keep in touch and check in with one another often to make sure you are all on the same page.

Fostering trust, open communication,
and a feeling of belonging in a blended family dynamic requires the creation of a secure environment. To create a secure place, consider the following ideas:

Communication that is Open and courteous: Promote communication that is both open and

Copyright ©

courteous among all family members. Make sure that everyone may share their ideas, emotions, and worries without worrying about being judged or criticized. Relationships may be strengthened and trust can be built by actively listening to each other and validating their viewpoints.

Establish Family Meetings:

Arrange frequent family gatherings so that everyone has the opportunity to voice their opinions, address any problems or obstacles, and work together to find solutions. These gatherings provide every family member a chance to speak out and actively contribute to the development of the family dynamic.

Establish Defined Expectations and Limits:

Define clearly defined expectations and limits for family members' conduct and duties. Make sure that everyone is aware of these expectations by communicating them clearly and concisely. A feeling of safety and structure is facilitated by consistency and justice in the enforcement of these limits.

Copyright ©

Encourage Emotional Expression:

Establish a setting that allows for honest and judgment-free emotional expression. Encourage family members to express their emotions and provide comfort and support to those who are struggling. This fosters emotional health and increases family trust.

Encourage individuality and inclusion by respecting and valuing the uniqueness, passions, and skills of each family member. Embrace everyone's interests and acknowledge their accomplishments. To promote a feeling of inclusion and belonging, include every family member in decision-making processes and family activities.

Practice dispute Resolution:

Teach and practice effective family dispute resolution techniques. Encourage family members to resolve disagreements amicably and constructively by emphasizing understanding one another's viewpoints and finding win-win solutions. Understanding how to handle conflicts fosters a feeling of safety and strengthens bonds between people.

Cultivate Quality Time:

Copyright ©

Make conscious efforts to spend time as a family in a quality manner. Plan family get-togethers, trips, or activities that everyone enjoys together. Creating happy memories and events increases the relationship between family members and fosters a feeling of community.

If difficulties with the mixed family dynamic continue or become too much to handle, think about getting professional assistance. Family therapists or counselors may provide direction, skills, and techniques made specifically for your situation to assist you get through any challenges.

Keep in mind that building a safe place is a continuous process that calls for all family members to be patient, empathetic, and actively involved. You may create a secure and caring atmosphere within your blended family by emphasizing open communication, respect for one another, and cultivating a feeling of belonging.

Copyright ©

Chapter 12

Early Recognizance of Red Flags

It's crucial to be able to see warning signals of a toxic relationship early on while dating as an older woman. This chapter will help you identify these red flags, comprehend the traits of a toxic relationship, and provide advice on how to leave one without risk. You may make wise decisions and foster wholesome and satisfying relationships by learning to recognize warning signs and giving your emotional health priority.

Signs

Lack of respect may be a sign of a toxic dynamic if your spouse frequently disregards your boundaries, ignores your thoughts, or minimizes your emotions.

Excessive possessiveness, jealousy, and efforts to control your conduct, relationships, or activities are

Copyright ©

all indications of controlling behavior, which may be a symptom of a toxic relationship.

Lack of Communication:
The basis of every successful relationship is communication. If your spouse habitually avoids direct dialogue or reacts defensively when you bring up problems, the relationship may not be healthy.

Manipulative conduct:
Constantly shifting the blame or engaging in manipulative conduct, such as guilt-tripping or gaslighting, is a huge warning sign. These strategies might damage your self-confidence and make it challenging to keep up a positive connection.

Extreme responses to trivial difficulties:
Extreme responses to trivial difficulties, unpredictable conduct, or sharp mood swings may be symptoms of emotional instability and might be a warning of a potentially toxic relationship.

Disregard for Your Well-Being:
If your spouse routinely prioritizes their needs and wants above yours or brushes off your worries, it

Copyright ©

may be an indication that they lack compassion and understanding.

Isolation from Loved Ones:
A toxic spouse can try to keep you away from your friends and family, which would make it more difficult for you to get outside assistance or keep up with connections.

Negative thought patterns:
Chronic negativity, pessimism, or continually making you feel bad may harm your emotional health and may be a sign of a toxic relationship.

Lack of Accountability:
In a happy marriage, both parties are accountable for their behavior. It may be a warning sign if your spouse continually refuses to accept responsibility for their actions or does not express regret after they have injured you.

Physical or Verbal Abuse:
Any instance of physical or verbal abuse, including intimidation, threats, or actual bodily injury, is very concerning and demands quick care.

Copyright ©

Telltale Symptoms of a Toxic Relationship

For your mental health, you must be aware of the warning signals that you are in a toxic relationship. Observe the warning indicators listed below:

Constant Emotional Drain:
If your relationship leaves you feeling emotionally spent, nervous, or on edge all the time, it may be a sign of a toxic dynamic that is harming your mental and emotional well-being.

Diminished Self-Worth:
Negative relationships may undermine your sense of self-worth and self-esteem. Being in a toxic relationship may be indicated if you often feel invalidated or doubt your worth.

Walking on Eggshells:
If you continually feel as if you need to be on your best behavior around your spouse or worry about how they will respond, this is a strong indication of an unhealthy and possibly poisonous relationship.

Loss of Independence:
Controlling relationships often restricts your freedom of action. A toxic relationship may be present if you start to lose sight of your objectives, passions, and sense of self.

Continual Cycle of Drama:
toxic relationships often include an ongoing drama cycle,
Drama often develops into a repeating pattern in unhealthy relationships. Here are some drama-related occurrences that might take place in a negative dynamic:

Volatile Arguments:
In toxic relationships, arguments often develop rapidly, become emotional, and include personal assaults. These debates often lack cooperative problem-solving and constructive communication.
Extreme emotional highs and lows are a hallmark of toxic partnerships. Periods of tremendous love and passion might be followed by abrupt changes to antagonism, rage, or retreat. This emotional rollercoaster may be demanding both physically and mentally.

Copyright ©

Constant Conflict:
Conflict becomes a constant in harmful partnerships. The relationship seems like a never-ending war, whether it's about little disagreements or more serious ones. Attempts to resolve the problem may be greeted with resistance or more conflict.

Manipulative Techniques:
Drama often results from one or both couples using manipulative techniques. These strategies may be used to influence and control the other person, such as guilt-tripping, mind games, or emotional blackmail.

magnified responses:
Small difficulties may be magnified in a toxic relationship, resulting in dramatic and exaggerated responses. Because of this, there may be tension and instability, and people may start to walk on eggshells more often.

Lack of Trust:
Trust is an essential element of every good relationship, but it is often undermined in toxic dynamics. Suspicion, resentment, and accusations can recur often, escalating the drama and hostility.

Copyright ©

Gossip and Betrayal:

In toxic relationships, members may engage in gossiping or disparaging remarks about one another in public or in private. This conduct may cause a breakdown in trust, more conflict, and more relationship harm.

Drama in unhealthy relationships often results from emotional manipulation. To exert control over and influence the other spouse's behavior or emotions, one partner may utilize guilt, fear, or emotional outbursts.

Conflicts are handled and resolved in good partnerships via open conversation and compromise. Conflicts, however, may go unsolved or come up again in toxic relationships because there is a lack of desire to settle problems and come to an agreement.

The drama may also take the form of attention-seeking behavior, in which one partner persistently looks to the other for approval, assurance, or pity. This conduct may result in a depleting dynamic centered on the person's unceasing craving for attention.

Copyright ©

It's important to consider if your relationship's drama cycle is healthy and sustainable for your well-being if you find yourself in it. Making effective changes begins with recognizing these habits.

Recognizing the signs of emotional abuse, emotional manipulation, and potential money diggers

Constant Criticism:

A person who abuses another person emotionally often engages in constant criticism of the victim, making derogatory comments about her appearance, abilities, or worth. They could minimize your achievements or instill insecurity in you.

To make you doubt your memory, perspective, or sanity, the perpetrator uses the psychological abuse tactic known as gaslighting, which distorts reality. They could change their minds about previous assertions or embellish the reality to cast doubt on their own experiences.

Copyright ©

Responsibility-Shifting:
People who misuse their emotions often shift the responsibility for their actions and their conduct onto others, including you. They could embellish the truth to cast blame on you or make you feel guilty for their mistakes.

Isolation:
Abusers often try to prevent their victims from contacting friends, relatives, or other supportive people. They could forbid you from visiting relatives or discourage you from doing so, making you dependent on them for social interaction and emotional support.

Control and Manipulation:
People who take advantage of your emotions can affect a wide range of aspects of your life. Your daily schedule might be dictated, your whereabouts monitored, your finances handled, or decisions made without taking into consideration your needs or involvement.

Abusers may utilize silent treatment or emotional withdrawal as a technique of punishment or social control. If they ignore you for an extended period or withhold their affection, you could feel scared, perplexed, and desperate for their attention.

Extreme jealousy and Possessiveness:
Extreme jealousy and possessiveness are warning signs of emotional abuse. An abuser may monitor your relationships, accuse you falsely of being unfaithful, or keep tabs on your friendships with people of the opposite sex.

Emotional Abuse:
Emotional abusers are skilled at preying on your feelings and exploiting your vulnerabilities. They could use your guilt, fear, or sympathy to manipulate you and get what they want.

Making You Believe Undeserving of Love, Respect, or Happiness: Abusers often make you believe that these things are not yours for the taking. They could constantly criticize you for your intelligence, abilities, or appearance, which eventually erodes your confidence.

Threats and intimidation:

Copyright ©

Threats of harm, violence, or destruction of property may sometimes accompany emotional abuse. Due to the climate of fear and control created by these threats, it becomes difficult to express oneself or exit the relationship.

It's important to remember that, regardless of age or gender, emotional abuse may occur in any form of relationship. Consider seeking advice and guidance from a trusted friend, family member, or knowledgeable person if any of these signs apply to your relationship.

Emotional abuse and manipulation:

Emotional abusers may exert control over their victims by using emotional blackmail. They could threaten to harm themselves or others, make you feel responsible for their sentiments, or take advantage of your emotions to get what they want.

Great Mood Swings:

Abusers often show great mood swings, going from being adoring and loving to enraged or hostile in a matter of seconds. You always have a sense of alertness and caution.

Lack of boundaries:

Copyright ©

Individuals who emotionally abuse you often disregard your boundaries, and if you try to enforce them, they could become angered or wounded. They could attempt to access your private accounts, read your conversations, or violate your privacy.

Withholding Love or Affection:

As a kind of punishment, persons in positions of control could refuse you their love or affection. To make you feel defenseless and dependent on their approval, they could restrict their affection, support, or physical touch from you.

Guilt is a powerful weapon that emotional abusers are experts at using to their advantage. They could try to make you feel guilty for making requests, engaging in hobbies, or taking time off. They twist the situation to make you seem uncaring or self-centered.

Copyright ©

Finding Prospective Gold Miners

Materialistic Focus:
A gold digger could be too interested in your wealth, possessions, or financial condition. They could place a higher value on lavish gifts, expensive trips, or your ability to support them than they would place on a genuine emotional connection.

Lack of Interest in Your Personal Life:
A money digger could not care about your plans, aspirations, or objectives. They could just be interested in material concerns and show no care for your emotional well-being or personal growth.

Financial dependence:
A gold digger may exhibit a pattern of financial dependence or reliance on others to preserve their way of life. The motivation or desire to labor for their financial stability may not exist in them.

Manipulative Behavior for Financial Gain:
Gold miners may pressure you into handing over money or other valuables by using dishonest

means. They may try to use guilt, flattery, or emotional blackmail to get you to give them money.

Interactions that are too shallow or superficial:

A gold digger may put more importance on appearances and monetary possessions than on compatibility or connection. They could place a higher value on monetary gain than in-depth talks or shared values.

It's important to remember that not everyone who has one or two of these traits is a manipulator, a money grab, or an emotional abuser. However, if you see a pattern of these behaviors in a relationship, it's important to examine the dynamics and consider seeking assistance or reassessing.

Unrealistic Lifestyle Expectations:

A gold digger may have extravagant lifestyle objectives that often include costly items, exotic vacations, and nonstop enjoyment. They could be quite clear about wanting you to pay for this way of life.

Lack of Reciprocity:
A gold digger often approaches relationships in a one-sided manner,

Copyright ©

focusing primarily on how they could financially profit from you. They can be hesitant to give their resources or make equivalent financial obligations.

Consistent Requests for Money:

If your spouse continually asks you for money, loans, or financial favors without displaying a genuine need or willingness to repay you, it may be a sign that they are a gold digger. They can rely on your financial support and put little effort into finding a solution to their financial issues.

Lack of Professional Motivation or Ambition:

Gold diggers often lack these traits. They may be content to rely on others for financial support rather than pursue their job or financial goals.

If your goals and ambitions are unconnected to making money, a gold digger may not be very interested in them. Your extracurricular activities, hobbies, and interests can be discounted or overlooked.

Copyright ©

Avoiding Financial Conversations:

A gold digger can try to avoid discussing money or making an awkward impression. They were unable to be open about their financial situation, and

When asked about their financial responsibilities or objectives, be evasive.

To learn about their past financial exploitation, look for parallels in their previous relationships. If they have a history of financially abusing others or have a repeating habit of wooing partners only for their financial wealth, it raises a red flag.

Prioritizing Material Things:

A gold digger could give top priority to possessions, appearance, and status symbols. They can be more interested in focusing on the financial security you can provide than they are in forging a deeper emotional connection or finding common ground.

Disregard for Personal Sacrifices:

If you make significant concessions or sacrifices for the relationship but the gold digger doesn't acknowledge them or show appreciation, it may be a sign that they are just interested in the financial advantages you can provide.

Copyright ©

Lack of Emotional Connection:

Gold diggers often only have a surface-level emotional connection, making it difficult for them to connect with someone. They could prioritize material gain before forging a strong, long-lasting bond.

It's important to keep in mind that these signs should be considered in conjunction with other pertinent considerations. It's crucial to trust your instincts and be honest with your partner about your expectations, convictions, and boundaries if you want to have a healthy and balanced relationship.

Symptoms of toxic relationships in advance and advice for avoiding them

Your ability to recognize the early warning signs of a toxic companion will determine how well you will fare. Below are some early warning signs of a toxic spouse and steps you may take to exit the relationship:

Early controlling behavior is a red flag if your spouse wants to keep you apart from your friends and family, restricts your social interactions, or keeps tabs on your whereabouts.

Jealousy and Possessiveness:

Excessive jealousy and possessiveness may be indications of dysfunctional dynamics. If your partner becomes excessively jealous of you or tries to control your interactions with others, toxic patterns of behavior may emerge.

Lack of respect:

A toxic spouse may minimize your feelings, ignore your ideas, or transgress your boundaries. They could slander you, call you names, or engage in other emotional abuse tactics.

One or more manipulative techniques include using mind games, guilt trips, or gaslighting as early signs of manipulation. A toxic partner may cloud your perception of reality, making you doubt your skills or prior experiences.

Copyright ©

Constant Criticism:

If your spouse constantly criticizes you, undermines your self-worth, or leaves you feeling inadequate, this might be a sign of toxic behavior. Feedback is advantageous in relationships with good partners, but it may be harmful to toxic ones.

Lack of Accountability: Risky partners often refuse to take responsibility for their actions. Because they could assign blame to someone else, provide explanations, or shirk responsibility, you can feel ignored and discarded.

Significant mood swings, which may vary from great fondness to sudden rage or hostility, may be an indication of toxic behavior. This volatility creates an unforeseen and unpredictable situation.

How to break up with a toxic partner

It might be difficult to leave a toxic relationship, but it's essential to put your health first and take back

Copyright ©

your happiness. Following are some ideas about how to leave a toxic relationship:

Recognize and acknowledge the relationship's toxicity and its negative effects on your emotional, mental, and physical health. Recognize that quitting the relationship is an essential step to finding happiness and rebuilding your self-esteem.

Seek Support:
Speak with dependable family members, friends, or a network of supporters who can provide emotional support during this trying time. Being around individuals who are concerned about your well-being may provide inspiration, direction, and perspective.

Create a strategy for securely terminating the relationship before you leave.
Consider contacting a professional, such as a counselor or advocate, who can assist you in creating a safety plan and providing resources, if you are concerned about any kind of violence or reprisal.

Set limits:

Clearly state and let your spouse know what those limits are. Make it clear that you demand respect for your decision to stop the relationship and be solid in your decision.

The best time and location to hold the chat are those that seem secure and comfortable for both of you. Choose a quiet, neutral area where you may speak freely without being interrupted or distracted.

Be straightforward and Firm:

When terminating the relationship, communicate straightforwardly and authoritatively. Avoid allowing the possibility for discussion or manipulation by being up forward about your choice to terminate the relationship.

Limit Contact:

It's crucial to restrict or stop communication with your toxic spouse once the relationship has ended. This can include preventing them from contacting you, unfollowing them on social media, and banning their phone number.

Copyright ©

Create a Support System:
Surround yourself with people who are uplifting and good influences. By getting in touch with friends, participating in support groups, or consulting a professional, you may strengthen your network of friends. You may find it easier to deal with the difficulties of exiting a toxic relationship if you have a solid support system.

Maintain Your Commitment:
Breaking up with a toxic spouse may be accompanied by times of uncertainty, loneliness, or even efforts by your ex to get you back. Remind yourself of the reasons you decided to leave the relationship and be steadfast in your choice. Keep in mind that you deserve to be in a happy and fulfilling relationship.

Finding the strength, bravery, and self-love necessary to leave a harmful relationship. You give yourself the best chance of finding a happier and more meaningful relationship in the future by prioritizing your health and taking the necessary action to break the toxic dynamic.

Copyright ©

Chapter 13

Advice for older ladies on online dating

Online dating has developed into a well-liked and practical method of meeting new people and pursuing prospective love relationships. The world of Internet dating may seem new or daunting to older women. The goal of this chapter is to provide insightful advice to assist older women get the most out of their online dating experience. You may improve your chances of discovering appropriate matches and forming deep relationships by being aware of the online dating scene and using smart tactics.

Selecting the Proper Platform

Not every dating site is made equally. When choosing an online dating site, take your dating objectives, tastes, and comfort level into account. Find a platform that supports older individuals and has features that meet your requirements by comparing several.

Developing an Interesting Profile

Your introduction to prospective mates is made via your online dating profile. Make a profile that showcases your special qualities and accurately represents who you are. Include a combination of appealing and current photographs as well as honest and fascinating facts about yourself.

Improving Communication Capabilities

When interacting with possible partners, effective communication is essential. Be careful with your vocabulary and tone, and put some work into crafting intelligent remarks that demonstrate a sincere interest in the recipient. To encourage interesting talks, use open-ended questions and pay close attention to their replies.

Setting reasonable goals

Set realistic expectations since online dating may be unpredictable. Recognize that enduring connections may not always result from every contact, and that's alright. Keep a cheerful attitude, maintain an open mind, and see every contact as a chance to improve.

Copyright ©

Using Online Safety Technique

When using an online dating site, security is of the utmost importance. Protect your private information, including your complete name, address, and credit card information. take trustworthy dating sites that place a high priority on user security, and take caution when disclosing personal information to prospective partners.

Dealing with Rejection

Online dating rejections are a normal part of the process. It's critical to cultivate resilience and refrain from taking rejection personally. Always keep in mind that compatibility is a matter of opinion, so it's preferable to concentrate on finding someone who respects you for who you are.

Going offline

Consider taking the relationship offline and scheduling a meeting if you've made a connection with someone. However, put your security first by meeting in a well-lit area and telling a reliable family member or friend about your intentions.

Following Your Gut Feelings

Copyright ©

Trust your gut as you navigate internet dating. Do not disregard your gut instincts if anything seems strange or raises questions. Put your safety and well-being first by cutting off any relationships or interactions that don't seem right.

Exercises in Patience
Finding the perfect partner requires time and patience. It's crucial to take your time and not jump into something before it's ready. Remain upbeat, enjoy the ride, and keep in mind that the ideal person can be waiting for you just around the corner.

Keeping a Balanced Diet
Finally, even though online dating might be exciting, it's important to keep your life in balance. Don't spend all of your time and energy on online dating. Maintain your current activities, your connections, and your emphasis on personal development.

Older women may confidently navigate the online world and improve their chances of making significant relationships by using this online dating advice. Always be loyal to who you are, be open to new options, and enjoy the process of meeting possible partners.

Copyright ©

Be Authentic:
In your online dating profile, present yourself genuinely and honestly. Avoid making false claims or posing as someone you're not. Honesty and trust are the foundations of real friendships.

Be Sophisticated:
Resist the urge to reply to every message or match that you get. Give each possible match careful consideration, and prioritize quality above quantity.

Be Open-Minded:
Be open-minded about people's backgrounds, hobbies, and ages. Give other folks a chance since you never know who you could connect with.

Use Filters Carefully:
To focus your search, make good use of the dating platform's search filters. This helps speed up the process of finding matches that fit your precise requirements.

Take care of yourself by taking vacations from online dating when necessary. Prioritize self-care and recharge if you are feeling overburdened or

Copyright ©

worn out before returning to the realm of online dating.

Be Patient with Technology:
There could be glitches and technical problems with online dating sites. Even if there are issues or you have trouble using the site, be patient and have a good outlook.

Meet in a Public Space:
Always choose a public area when meeting someone for the first time. Consider telling a friend or family member about your intentions and making travel arrangements to and from the meeting location.

Believe Your Gut:
When interacting with a possible match, if anything seems odd or makes you feel uneasy, believe your gut. When determining if a relationship is healthy and real, your intuition may be a powerful guide.

Take it Slow: Resist the urge to get into a relationship right away. Before seeking a deeper commitment, take the time to slowly get to know someone and build a strong foundation of trust and compatibility.

Copyright ©

Learn from your experiences:
View every conversation and date as a chance for personal development. Think back on your experiences, figure out what works for you, and modify your strategy as necessary.

Keep a Positive Attitude:
Although online dating may sometimes be depressing, it's crucial to keep a positive attitude. Do not allow failures or rejections to depress you. Maintain a positive mindset and have faith that a fulfilling relationship might be discovered.

Enjoy Yourself:
Dating online ought to be a fun and exciting experience. Accept the challenge, go into it with a sense of humor, and don't forget to enjoy yourself.

Remember that there are other ways to meet possible mates than internet dating. Don't restrict yourself to depending just on online channels. Take part in hobbies and social gatherings that suit your interests to increase your chances of meeting others who share your interests. Enjoy getting to know

Copyright ©

people, and have faith that the proper connection will materialize when it does.

Engaging Messages and Navigating Online Conversations real-world examples.

Personalize Your Messages: Read the other person's profile attentively and make sure to emphasize anything in particular that caught your attention. This shows your genuine interest in getting to know them.
Example: "Hello Ben, I can tell from looking at your profile that you like hiking. I have discovered a lovely path nearby. Have you been there before?

Utilize Open-Ended Questions:
utilize open-ended questions to encourage meaningful dialogues and elicit more information than a simple "yes" or "no" response. This facilitates getting to know one another and makes dialogue simpler to follow.

For instance, "Sarah, I notice you like photography. What sparked your desire to document life's moments? Do you have a favorite topic that you like to photograph?

To help people connect with you, add a sense of fun to your conversations. An enjoyable atmosphere may be created with a great joke or witty discussion. Using Mike as an example, the exchange would be as follows: Your humorous bio made me smile nonstop. It seems that we have similar senses of humor. What was the funniest thing that occurred to you lately, please?

Share Personal Narratives:

Talking about your own life experiences and stories allows you to be open, honest, and vulnerable. The other person may feel more connected as a result and be motivated to share their own stories.

"Karen, I recently traveled to Italy and had the most amazing food adventure," as an illustration. Have you ever been somewhere where the food made a lasting impact on your palate?

Copyright ©

Show genuine interest in the other person's comments and actively listen to what they have to say. Active listening and responding. In your response, be kind and refer to particular points they mentioned to show that you are paying attention to what they are saying.

For instance, say, "David, I appreciate your perspective on mindfulness and meditation. I've been trying to incorporate more mindfulness practices into my daily routine. Do you have any tips for beginners?"

Be courteous and Polite:

Always use a courteous tone while communicating. Avoid contentious or delicate subjects, and be nice and considerate to the other person.

I'd love to learn more about the causes you're interested in and how they've touched your life, for instance: "Hi Emily, I hope you're having a great day. Your passion for volunteering is inspiring."

Don't Be Afraid to Flirt:

If the chat is going well and you sense a connection, don't be afraid to flirt with your messages. However, be considerate of the other person's level of comfort and make sure the flirting is lighthearted and amusing.

James, the grin on your profile photo is infectious and it made my day. Would you mind sharing the secret to that radiant smile?

Respect Boundaries:

Pay attention to any indications of boundaries made by the other person. Respect their comfort zone and shift the topic of the discussion if they are reluctant to provide specific personal details.

Using Julia as an example, the speaker may say, "Julia, I sense that discussing family might be a sensitive topic for you. Please know that I'm here to listen and talk about whatever you feel comfortable sharing."

Take Charge:

If the connection is solid and both sides are at ease, don't be hesitant to take the lead and recommend taking the conversation from the online platform to a phone call or in-person encounter.

It would be fantastic to hear your voice, Ryan, and I have liked our discussions so far. Would you be open to talking on the phone sometime?"

Copyright ©

Last but not least, believe in your instincts. Trust your gut feelings and use care if anything seems strange or if you see any warning signs. Always put your security and well-being first.

As an example, try saying, "Rachel, I've had a great time getting to know you, but I noticed a few inconsistencies in your stories. I believe in being open and honest in any relationship, so I wanted to address my concerns. Can we have an open conversation about this?"

Show Genuine Interest:

By asking follow-up questions and actively participating in the discussion, show genuine interest in the other person. This demonstrates your respect for their ideas and viewpoints.

As an example, "Mark, I noticed that you enjoy playing the guitar. How did you first get into it? Do you have a favorite genre or artist you like to play?"

Be positive and friendly:

Maintain a positive and friendly tone in your communications. Positivity is contagious and may create a nice atmosphere for both parties.

Consider this: Lisa here. Your profile indicates that you like traveling, which I can tell. What is your

Copyright ©

most treasured travel experience to date? I'd be curious to learn more.

Search for shared pleasures or interests in order to establish a connection.

It is easier to connect with someone who shares your interests or hobbies.

For instance: "Andrew, I notice you like to cook, and I'm constantly searching for new recipes to try. Recently, have you tried any new ones?

Be yourself because authenticity is crucial. In your discussions, be sincere and let your personality shine through. Try not to pretend to be someone you're not since genuine friendships are built on honesty.

Exercise Patience:

It could take some time before an internet argument gains traction. Being patient and giving the other person time to respond is important. Never rush the process or exert pressure on them.

Such is, "Hey Michael, hope you're having a nice week. I was just wondering if you have any fun plans for the weekend. I simply wanted to say hello, no hurry.

Emoticons and GIFs may add a whimsical touch to your communications. Use them to lighten the tone. They could assist you in expressing your goals and giving your speeches personality.
"Hello Sarah," for instance I wanted to let you know how much I loved watching this adorable dog GIF and I hope it made your day as well!

Be Privacy Aware:
Sharing and networking are essential, but be cautious about sharing too much personal information. Maintain your privacy and only provide information when you feel at ease doing so.

End Conversations Positively:
By expressing your happiness with the conversation, you may set a pleasant tone for future interactions.
Believing that the right person will come into your life at the right time requires trusting the process and accepting that not every contact will end in a perfect match. Instead, appreciate the journey and enjoy the relationships you form.
For example, "Alex, I've enjoyed talking to you and I appreciate your honesty," See where our journey takes us as we learn to know one another better.

Copyright ©

Enjoy the ride, be true to yourself, and remember that the perfect person is out there waiting to meet you. By adopting these suggestions and real-world examples, you may handle online chats with confidence and boost your chances of making significant connections.

How to recognize bogus internet frauds with examples of how to do so

To protect yourself from loss of money and possible danger, it's critical to recognize false internet frauds. Here are some concrete instances and tips:

Look for poor grammar, spelling mistakes, or generic greetings as these can be indicators of a scam. Suspicious Emails or Messages: Be wary of unsolicited emails or messages that request personal information, financial information, or passwords. Scammers may impersonate trustworthy organizations or people to trick you into disclosing sensitive information.

Example: You get an email purporting to be from a bank requesting you to send your login details or account information via a supplied link because your account has been hacked. Reputable institutions would never request such information through email.

Pay attention to the website's URL as scammers may use slight variations or misspellings of legitimate domain names. Look for secure website indicators, such as a padlock icon in the browser's address bar. Phishing Websites: Scammers frequently create fake websites that mimic legitimate ones to trick users into entering their personal or financial information.

Example: You click on a link in an email that purports to be from a well-known online business, but the website you arrive at asks you to submit your credit card information to get a great discount but has a different URL and no security signs.

Look for inconsistencies in their profile information, such as conflicting details or overly flattering language. Reverse image searches their profile picture to see if it was stolen from someone else's online presence. Fake profiles on social media or dating sites: Scammers create fake profiles to

Copyright ©

develop emotional connections with people and then exploit them for financial gain.

Example: You meet an attractive person on a dating site who claims to have a high-paying job, and a luxurious lifestyle, and shows great affection for you early on. They ultimately ask for money, stating different justifications like a medical emergency or financial trouble.

Lottery or Prize Scams:

Be wary of unsolicited emails or phone calls claiming you have won a large sum of money or a valuable prize. Scammers may ask for payment for processing fees, taxes, or other expenses to release their winnings. Reputable lotteries and contests do not demand you to pay upfront to claim your prize.

Example: You get a call congratulating you on winning a luxurious vacation package, but before you can collect your prize, they want a substantial upfront payment to cover administrative costs and taxes.

Investment Opportunities with Unrealistic Returns:

Be wary of investment opportunities that claim to offer unusually high returns or profits that are guaranteed with little risk;

Copyright ©

con artists may pressure you to invest quickly without providing adequate information.

A "once-in-a-lifetime" investment opportunity with guaranteed returns of 200% in a matter of months is advertised by email or phone, urging you to act quickly and transfer cash without giving any paperwork or a thorough explanation of how the investment works.

Techniques involving pressure and urgency:

Scammers often use pressure and urgency to push you into making snap judgments. They may do this by invoking fear, making threats, or providing time-sensitive offers to get you to act without thinking.

Example: You get a message or call stating that your bank account has been hacked and that you must instantly submit your personal information to stop future harm as failing to do so would have serious repercussions.

Request for Payment Using Untraceable Methods:
Scammers often demand payment using untraceable means, like wire transfers, prepaid gift cards, or cryptocurrencies, which make it difficult to retrieve cash after they have been transferred.

Copyright ©

As an example, a vendor on an online marketplace may insist on payment through wire transfer or cryptocurrency rather than a more safe and traceable method, all the while making up a story about a "special discount."

Safety Measures for Online Meetings with Strangers

Prioritizing your safety and well-being while meeting new people offline is crucial if you're an older woman trying out dating. Offline interactions are thrilling and potentially rewarding, but they also have certain hazards that must be appropriately addressed. You may navigate the dating world with assurance and peace of mind by taking safety precautions and adhering to safety rules.

This chapter is dedicated to teaching you important safety measures while meeting new people offline. These recommendations are made expressly for older women in mind who are looking for friendship and deep relationships in mind. These safety precautions can help you maintain your security whether you're meeting someone for the first time or moving from online talks to in-person encounters.

While the majority of individuals you encounter will be genuine, it's crucial to keep in mind that you should constantly exercise care and awareness. You may reduce dangers and provide a safer atmosphere for yourself by adopting these safety measures into your dating life.

Every precaution, from picking proper meeting spots to telling a reliable friend about your intentions, is meant to give you the capacity to make wise choices and safeguard your well-being. Keep in mind that your safety is of the utmost importance, and it's crucial to trust your gut and take the necessary precautions to guarantee a happy and secure dating experience.

We will discuss some safety measures for meeting new individuals offline in the sections that follow. These recommendations will provide you with the information and resources you need to effectively navigate the dating scene and establish relationships while maintaining your safety. Let's dig in and examine the steps that will help older women have a safer and more satisfying experience while dating.

Copyright ©

Your intuition is a great tool, so trust it. Trust your intuition and use care if anything seems wrong or causes you to have questions.

Meet in a Public Space:
Pick a busy, well-lit public area when meeting someone for the first time. The best locations to feel safe and at ease are coffee shops, restaurants, and parks.

Before meeting someone offline, tell a friend or family member you can trust about your intentions. Give specifics like the person's name, the time, and the place. It's always useful to have someone know where you are.

Utilize Your Transportation:
It is recommended to utilize your means of transportation while going on a date. This gives you control over your movement and guarantees that you may leave the area at any moment, should you need to.

Keep Your Personal Information Private:
Don't divulge too much about yourself too early in a dating relationship. Don't provide your home

address, location of employment, or financial information until you have built up some trust with the individual.

Set limits:
Be upfront with your prospective spouse about your expectations and limits. The dating process should be enjoyable and respectful for both parties.

Limit alcohol intake during the first meetings to keep your mind sharp and stay mindful of your surroundings. Controlling your senses enables you to stay safe and make wise judgments.

Carry a Phone and Keep It Charged:
Keep your phone with you at all times, fully charged, and within reach. This guarantees that you may ask for assistance if necessary.

Choose a reliable emergency contact to serve as your point of contact. Give the person you're meeting their contact information, and advise your emergency contact of your intentions.

Practice Safe Online Communication:
Before meeting someone in person, be sure you've spoken with them online long enough to build trust.

Copyright ©

Check for consistency in their behaviors and determine if their words and deeds line up.

Slow Down:
Don't rush into private or delicate situations at first. Permit trust and understanding to grow gradually throughout the partnership.

Meet During the Day:
Choose daytime meetings, particularly for the first sessions. Environments during the day are often safer and provide more sight.
Keep a watch on your things, including your pocketbook, phone, and other priceless items. Keep children from being left alone or in danger.

Reliable Friends as Wingwomen:
Make plans for a friend to be there throughout your date, if at all feasible. To make sure you're comfortable and secure, they may quietly watch from a distance or even participate in some of the dates.

Follow Your Own Pace:
Only continue the connection if you feel at ease and prepared to do so. Do not feel compelled to

Copyright ©

participate in endeavors or circumstances with which you are not familiar.

Keep in mind that while meeting new individuals offline, your safety comes first. You may enjoy dating with peace of mind by adhering to these safety guidelines. Trust yourself, put yourself first, and take the necessary precautions to make sure your travel is safe and pleasurable.

Copyright ©

For older ladies seeking for a lifelong spouse, here is one more bit of advice

Keep in mind that age is only a number and that your heart knows no bounds as you embark on your search for a life partner. Accept the wisdom and insights that come with experience, and let them point you in the direction of a deep, enduring love. Here are a few suggestions to keep you inspired along the way:

Age constraints are invisible to love, which is simply aware of the boundless potential of the union of two souls.

Unknown source: "True love is not about finding someone who completes you, but about finding someone who celebrates and enhances the beautiful completeness you already possess."

Believe in the power of love because it has the ability to fascinate people at any stage of life. You

Copyright ©

could come across the love story of a lifetime if you embrace the voyage with an open heart.

We often find the most amazing relationships when we least expect them.

"Remember that you deserve a love that honors and values each stage of your life. Your advanced years are proof of your perseverance, fortitude, and life experience.

Therefore, my dear older women, remember that the hunt for love has no age restrictions. The perfect partner is out there waiting who will appreciate and love you for who you are, so keep your heart open, be sincere with yourself, and have trust in that. Your age is not a restriction, but rather a monument to the magnificent life you have lived; the love that is waiting for you may be the cherry on top of your journey.

The depth of the connection and the bond created by the union of two souls, rather than age, are what define love.

Copyright ©

Every occasion is an opportunity to create wonderful memories with a partner for life, and every second is a chance for love to grow.

Every chapter in the tapestry of love stories that is life has the promise of a new beginning. Recognize your options and let love write a fantastic tale for you.

The benefit of falling in love later in life is that you have the perspective to recognize its value, the stamina to nurture it, and the knowledge to make it endure forever.

A force that transcends space and time allows two souls to connect deeply and transformatively.

Never let time cause your belief in love to fade. Your heart knows what it wants, and it will lead you to the love story that was meant for you.

"You are a testimony to your age in terms of beauty and toughness. Love should be the crowning

Copyright ©

achievement of your extraordinary journey, so accept it, take pleasure in it, and let it lead you.

"Love is everlasting, and at any age, it has the power to alter the direction of your life. Profit from the ability to create a love story that is only yours.

Accept the journey, believe in the power of love, and allow your heart to lead you to a relationship that brings you pleasure, company, and a profound sense of connection. The romantic tale you deserve is waiting for you, eager to start in the most lovely and surprising manner. Your advanced years are a tribute to your unfathomable power and knowledge.

Copyright ©

Thanks for Reading

Printed in Great Britain
by Amazon